Dear Ann and Lorey,
Wishing you and yours the Very
Best from Wolfcrest,
Love,
Pat

Denholms

Patricia A. Wolf
12/19/2011

Denholms

THE STORY OF WORCESTER'S
PREMIER DEPARTMENT STORE

CHRISTOPHER SAWYER & PATRICIA A. WOLF

Charleston · London

THE
History
PRESS

Published by The History Press
Charleston, SC 29403
www.historypress.net

All images are from the authors' collections unless otherwise noted.

First published 2011

Manufactured in the United States

ISBN 978.1.60949.395.0

Sawyer, Christopher.
Denholms : the story of Worcester's premier department store / Christopher Sawyer and
Patricia A. Wolf.
p. cm.
Includes bibliographical references.
ISBN 978-1-60949-395-0
1. Denholm & McKay Co. (Worcester, Mass.)--History. 2. Department stores--
Massachusetts--Worcester--History. I. Wolf, Patricia A. II. Title.
HF5465.U64D467 2011
381'.141097443--dc23
2011042017

Notice: The information in this book is true and complete to the best of our knowledge. It is offered without guarantee on the part of the authors or The History Press. The authors and The History Press disclaim all liability in connection with the use of this book.

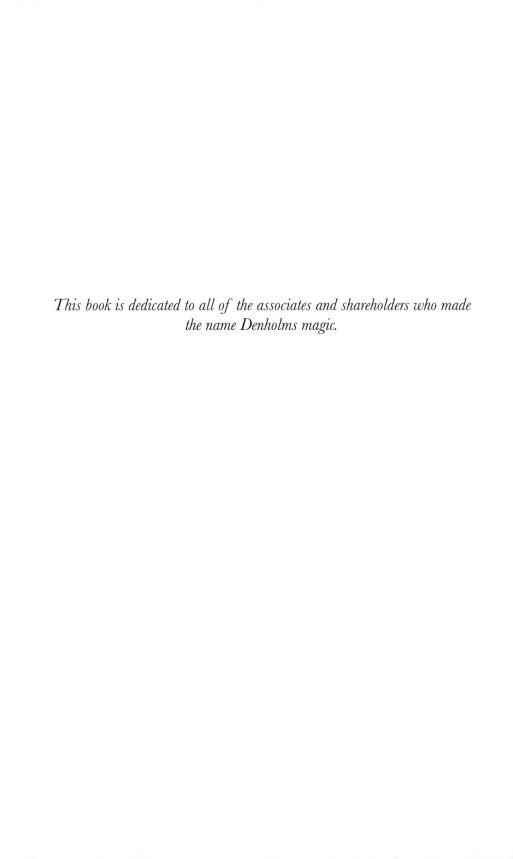

This book is dedicated to all of the associates and shareholders who made the name Denholms magic.

Contents

Acknowledgements

Several people helped with the writing of this book, and many new friendships were formed. We would like to take the time to thank all of you who wrote in their stories or conversed over the phone to relive your days at Denholms. The authors would like to say a special thank-you to the Harry Wolf family, the Russell Corsini family, Mr. and Mrs. Eric Hallback, Carol Sawyer, the archives of Josephine Carbone, Ted Coghlin, Lillian Gordon and the *Worcester Telegram and Gazette*, as well as Bob Branczyk and Irving Bostock for supplying imagery and memories.

Introduction

S ome of us will never forget the department stores of our youth. These were grand structures that anchored any given downtown shopping district. These stores were also intertwined with significant milestones in our lives—our visit with Santa, shopping for a new Easter hat, purchasing a wedding gown or simply marveling at the elaborate window displays during the Christmas season. In Worcester, that store was the Denholm and McKay Company, simply known as Denholms. Denholms was the leader of the Worcester downtown area and the grande dame of Main Street. With its six floors (seven including the basement), it was Worcester's largest and most modern department store. Specializing in up-to-the-minute fashion trends while keeping a family-friendly environment, the store always remained true to its founding principal that quality, fashion and value can happily coexist while maintaining a high level of customer service.

Denholms was located in the heart of the Commonwealth and in the hearts of its patrons and employees. We hope that this book stirs up some of your own memories of Denholms, and we look forward to sharing ours with you.

Chapter 1
The Birth of an Industry

In the 1870s, Worcester, Massachusetts, was a city on the verge of change. The Industrial Revolution was in its early stages, and Worcester had been a vital contributor to the new advances being made since 1856. Great factories were continually opening up, replacing farmland and dirt-ridden streets. These immense brick buildings, with their soot-laden windows, heavy machinery and smokestacks, manufactured such everyday items as barbed wire, leather footwear and corsetry for the masses.

With the addition of all these new jobs came the need for more employees, and they came in droves. Large masses of immigrants from Italy, Poland and Ireland migrated to the newly formed city in search of work. Among these immigrants was a large population of women who worked in the factories, primarily the Worcester Corset Factory, the various textile looms and the production of Valentine cards started by Ester Howland. All these newly founded jobs gave hope and prosperity to a growing workforce and helped to stimulate the second-largest city outside of Boston.

Due to a lack of housing, newly formed triple-deckers were soon being erected (primarily for the workforce). Made out of timber and brick, they were modest in their design but helped to house more people in a smaller footprint. Located within walking distance of the downtown area, they helped to form new neighborhoods consisting of varied ethnic and social backgrounds. Factory owners also lived in these new housing developments and often rented out upper floors to the workers whom they employed.

These newly formed industries were not established by themselves. It took great men with a vision for the future to see what the masses wanted to consume. They were men from all walks of life. Some were locals, and some traveled from distant countries to start new lives for themselves and their families. But what they all had in common was the idea to capitalize on a growing consumer base whose immigration to the States was at an alarming pace. They knew they could find workers to help assist with their new inventions, and they were almost guaranteed consumption by the U.S. market.

One such entrepreneur was William Alexander Denholm. Denholm, who was born in Dundee, Scotland, on May 8, 1837, was the son of John and Jessie Milne Denholm. John Denholm worked for the Scottish Iron Foundry for all of his adult years, and his wife was a stay-at-home mother who tended to the family. At the young age of thirteen, William Alexander Denholm attended middle school in the city of Glasgow, where he excelled at mathematics and English studies. At that age, the young William lost his father when he died suddenly. The elder Denholm's death forced the young student to leave school and take up work to help support his family. His first position was with a linen establishment based in Glasgow. Denholm worked hard during his entry to the company, learning the manufacturing and operational duties that came with the position. He was also keenly interested in how the whole business operated on every level. Learning the retail trade was an exciting and new opportunity for him to advance to a higher level of management. By the age of twenty, he had been promoted to resident buyer for Robert Struthers, a linen company also based in Glasgow. This job allowed him travel to the States—primarily New York City. Denholm liked the city and everything that it had to offer, including a faster pace, worldwide trading and the possibility of growth. Soon after his trip to the States, he returned to his homeland to continue work, but his stay would be brief.

Denholm longed to move back to New York to further his career. He landed a new position with the firm of Linder, Kingsley & Company, known for being in the wholesale trade of fine linens and embroideries. Most of this was based out of the New York dwelling where the company was incorporated. To stay close to the business, Denholm took up residence in Williamsburg, Brooklyn, where he lived for the first seven years after arriving in the States. During that time, he met Grace McLay, who was also born in Glasgow. The two wed in New York on a warm summer day in August 1859. Soon after, the newlyweds made the decision to move to the Passaic region of New Jersey, where they lived for another five years. The couple planned to start a family, and soon after, their first child was born. Her name was Elizabeth, and she was born in Williamsburg, New York, on March 14, 1861. Their second child, Jessie Miln, was born on August 23, 1864. The third addition to the family was young William, who died in infancy while the couple was residing in New Jersey. Grace, who was their fourth child, was born on April 20, 1869.

The cost of living in the big city was getting too expensive for William and his growing family, and he longed to move north. He had heard about the Industrial Revolution that was taking place in Worcester, Massachusetts, with its factories and large production capabilities. Denholm was intrigued by the influx of people relocating to downtown Worcester and realized the growth and potential the new city could have for himself and his family. He made up his mind, and he and the family packed up and relocated to the new city. It was the start of a new chapter in their lives, and dreams of prosperity fueled their desire.

Chapter 2
A Store Is Born

In 1870, after arriving in Worcester, Denholm was reassured that he had made the right decision to relocate there. Streets were bustling with employees of the factories, as well as patrons who lived in the large mansions near the city. Transportation by railroad made Worcester an easy destination, and various merchants began opening up shops trying to compete for the consumers' dollars. By 1870, the population of Worcester had grown to 41,105 as more people began to immigrate to Worcester in search of work.[1] At that time, William Denholm partnered with William C. McKay to go into business for themselves. McKay, who was born in Kingston, Ontario, was a resident of Boston employed at Churchill, Watson & Company. Churchill was a dry goods store located in the heart of downtown Boston. (A dry goods store at that time was one that primarily sold textiles, notions and clothing.) Denholm was confident that his partnership with McKay could fill a retail gap in the heart of Worcester.

The pair knew that other large stores had established themselves downtown, including the Barnard and Sumner Company (later called Barnard, Putnam and Sumner), as well as the company of Finlay, Lawson & Kennedy. Finlay, Lawson & Kennedy was at that time looking to get out of the retail trade and was up for sale. Denholm and McKay bought the assets and the location at the corner of Main and Mechanics Streets and began to plan for their new venture. The store opened in November 1870 to great fanfare. The contents were that of your typical dry goods store of that time, as well as various items not readily available in that marketplace. But many new innovations set the pair apart from the competition. Among the many changes the pair made was that of fair and fixed pricing. During that time, stores would often mark tickets with codes to see how much they could get the consumer to spend, or else the practice of bartering would take place to make a sale. The concept of fixed pricing was a rather new innovation and widely adopted in larger cities such as Boston. Therefore, the term "Boston Store" was added to the Denholm and McKay signage and advertising to make customers aware that they were getting a fair and honest deal. Another first was the decision to stay open only one night a week, primarily Saturday. Up to that point, retailers had been open for business seven nights a week. Soon after the success of Denholm and McKay, other stores followed suit, and common business hours were adopted by the city's shopping districts.

The original store was modest in comparison to what it would become. With its large, striped awnings that framed out the arched window displays,

Denholm and McKay Company, Main and Mechanics Street, 1870. *From the collections of the Worcester Historical Museum, Worcester, Massachusetts.*

showcasing the various merchandise and trimmings popular with the Worcester consumer, along with the new pricing policy, it was no wonder the company found success. At opening, the pair employed eighteen associates, with Denholm and McKay doing the entire bookkeeping, ordering and managing. Within a few years, sales were increasing at an alarming pace, and future growth was inevitable. Given the present location, expansion was not possible. With the inability to expand up or out, the decision was made to seek new quarters for the firm.

Chapter 3
Clark's New Block

B y 1880, the Denholm and McKay dry goods store had outgrown its present address. A search was on to find a new location where the pair could expand their offerings and still have room to grow. At that time, Jonas G. Clark approached the two businessmen with the prospect of building a new store specially designed for them.

Clark, who was a wealthy businessman, was born twenty miles outside of Worcester in the town of Hubbardston, Massachusetts. He was an entrepreneur based in San Francisco who dealt with importing various products out of the West Coast. Eventually, his trading became limited to furniture, and within a few years, he found himself in the manufacturing and distribution of high-end furniture. It wasn't long before Clark had amassed a handsome return on his investment and decided to liquidate his business and move back to the East Coast. Residing in New York City on the fashionable upper Fifth Avenue, he got involved in the real estate market. That venture took him to Worcester with the idea to broaden his investments into the commercial side of the market. Worcester was the perfect location to erect the buildings that Clark had envisioned, and the duo of Denholm and McKay were the perfect tenants for his venture.

Some merchants at the time were skeptical about the proposed new store being built in the South Main part of town, but Denholm and McKay were confident in their new location. The parcel was located directly across from city hall and at the end of Franklin Street, giving it direct exposure to anyone coming into town. And for Clark, it was a plot of land large enough to house his new building in the manner in which he wanted it constructed. Clark hired the architectural firm of Earle and Fuller to carry out the design and construction. Stephan Earle was a local resident, born and raised in Leicester and schooled at Boston's MIT. Years later, he traveled to Europe to further his design skills and eventually returned to New England, where he joined forces with James Fuller and the duo started their own design firm.

The building Earle and Fuller designed for Clark spared no expenses. The new structure would be five stories high with a grand center tower. The façade would be 180 feet wide on the Main Street side and would consist of red brick with terra cotta and limestone accents. Heavy uses of ornamental accents punctuated the design, from the grand column and roofline to the details around the main entrances. Large banks of leaded-glass windows covered the main body of the building, while smaller showcase windows anchored the entrance. As a finishing touch, a wrought-iron railing would be installed to cap off the structure, with a flag waving proudly on the column.

The interior of the building was at the time the most modern and up-to-date in the city of Worcester. Oak and mahogany were used throughout the space as flooring and wall trim, and each floor was wired completely for telephone usage by running the wires up the main center column to keep them out of view from the public. The upper floors (two through five) were primarily devoted to office space, and many prominent businessmen soon signed contracts to lease this most modern building. Among them was the architectural firm of Earle and Fuller. The main floor and basement were reserved for the Denholm and McKay Company, alongside a small millinery shop and an insurance company.

Great waves of fanfare and anxiety erupted as the date approached for the opening of the new structure. At that time, most commercial and residential space was lit by gas lamps. Gas lamps were unpredictable at times and created soot, which covered walls and ceilings along with any merchandise in the vicinity. Clark chose to have his building wired for electricity from top to bottom and installed a self-sufficient electrical plant in the rear of the structure. Electricity was a fairly new innovation at that time, and several residents were skeptical of the new invention, fearing fire or, worse, shock to themselves. A petition was soon signed and passed on to the city council but was largely ignored and overruled before the opening.

In September 1882, the new store was opened. The building was widely praised for its design and amenities, including four passenger elevators and four main staircases, allowing customers and workers greater access to the upper floors. The business of Denholm and McKay in its new territory was an instant hit with customers. Wide, spacious aisles with new mahogany and glass case lines formed neatly presented statements. The offerings were expanded to include a small array of home furnishings and textiles, as well as an expanded assortment of lace and trimmings. Most women at the time were still making their own clothes, and the expanded assortment was a welcome addition. All these enhancements brought in greater revenue for the duo, but the excitement would be short-lived. For the time being, the pair was sure they had made the right decision, and increasing profits and sales reassured them.

On May 7, 1884, Mr. McKay passed away suddenly, and a change in procedure was inevitable. Denholm and McKay had both signed an agreement that stated, "If either partner shall die during the continuance of this agreement, the other party shall carry on the business in the same manner until the next stock taking, and the survivor shall have the option of taking the assets himself, at such terms as may be agreed upon by the legal representatives of the deceased and himself, or put the business into liquidation for the benefits of both parties."[2] William McKay had drafted a will in earlier years and made Denholm his sole executor. To appease the McKay family and his widow, Margaret McKay, Denholm took a full inventory of the store and its assets, and appraisers were on hand to assure the probate court that all necessary steps were being taken to purchase the McKay share of the business at fair market value. After many revisions by the probate court, it was decided to continue the corporation, and Denholm formed a partnership with Robert J. McKay (William's eldest brother). Denholm alone would maintain controlling interest in the business.

Over the next few years, the business grew at an alarming pace, and customers clamored for more inventories to purchase. The firm of

Denholm and McKay was rapidly buying up vacated office space to expand its offerings and had taken over the entire first floor, as well as the second and third. Growth was inevitable, and Worcester consumers were growing more anxious and demanding in what they desired. Along with that growth came a need for a more structured management team. Denholm appointed Robert McKay as his chief secretary and enlisted John Hughes to be assistant manager. Having a management team in place allowed Denholm to grow the business without having to manage its daily duties and responsibilities. Denholm also included his new management team in the various legal and corporate documents and prepared to hand the business over in case of death.

With a need for greater buying power to fill the store and offer the goods that its consumers wanted, the Denholm and McKay Company joined the Syndicated Trading Company as a charter member. As one of its earliest members, Denholm and McKay was alongside such great companies as Forbes and Wallace of Springfield, the Minneapolis Dry Goods and various other Scottish-founded stores. The trading company was formed by Abel Swan Brown to assist smaller companies with the ability to buy greater commodities at a lower price while purchasing

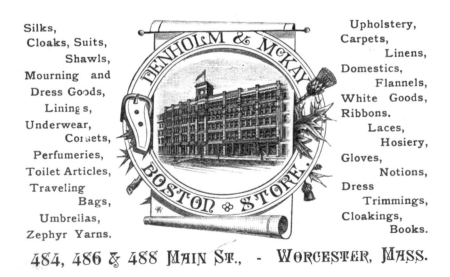

An advertising postcard, circa 1900.

in bulk. With offices in New York City, Paris, Germany and England, the team was in the center of the retail community and could travel to Europe with ease. The ability to buy goods not usually offered at the time helped the Denholm and McKay Company fulfill its expansion and offer new and exciting imports to its customers, many of which had not been seen before. With a passion and excitement for what was happening in the Worcester market, A. Swan Brown purchased a controlling interest in the Denholm and McKay Company and was made vice-president within the management team. Now Swan had a say in all executive decisions, as well carrying out various buying and sourcing duties from his office in New York City.

The Passing of the Torch

On March 28, 1891, another tragedy came sooner than expected. William A. Denholm died from a weakening of his heart due to anemia. News of his death created widespread sorrow in the business community, as well as in the heart of Worcester. Denholm had been seen as a great leader in society and had involved himself with various church and civic causes and become a pillar of the community. His death marked a major change in the way the business would be run. Within twenty years of opening, both Denholm and McKay had passed on, and it was time for a new regime.

In 1897, the junior partners settled with the Denholm estate and formed the Denholm and McKay Company with Abel Swan as its president and his brother Irving Swan Brown as vice-president. This was the largest clearing sale in the history of Worcester, and it enabled the partners to purchase the business and have it incorporated under the laws of the states. At that time, more than $500,000 had been paid in capital to form the new corporation. Incorporating the business gave the partners more ease for cash flow and a chance to borrow more heavily to grow the business. At the same time, the electrical plant that had once provided electricity to the building was expanded in the rear of the basement and now supplied electricity to the whole block under the new Denholm and McKay Electrical Company. What had started out as twenty-five thousand square feet on the first and lower-level floors now occupied most of the building up to the fifth floor. Expansion was needed to grow the business further.

In 1906, the Denholm and McKay Company purchased the Clark building under the newly formed Denholm and McKay Realty Trust

A postcard showing original annex, circa 1916.

and set out for expansion up to High Street. A newly formed annex was built, with a walkway connecting the two buildings. During the next year, the Denholm and McKay Company purchased most of the remaining offices in the building and turned them into selling space. Now "Clark's block" had been formally taken over by the company, and a two-story marquee was erected on top of the center column, stating "The Boston Store." This was central Massachusetts's largest store, employing 450 associates, and the largest outside Boston.

Interior enhancements were made to better suit the new store, including an enlargement of the staircase leading to upper floors, allowing for better passage. Interior firewalls made of large steel panels with rivets were erected to help protect in case of an accident or fire to the newly formed departments. These doors slid behind existing walls and were completely hidden from view when not in use. The former basement doors were bricked up, and new and larger ones were formed to allow easy access for the trade and display of household items such as utensils, appliances, silverware and Japanese goods. The first floor was broken up into specific departments selling cotton and wool fabric, notions, dress trimmings and lace. Various other dry goods were nestled between a newly formed boot and shoe department, hosiery, men's and women's gloves, books and stationery. On the second floor, millinery, cloaks, suits and women's foundations sat next to newly formed offices of the management team. The third floor consisted of carpeting and upholstery goods, rugs, mattings, window curtains and draperies, shades and light fixtures. The fourth floor was converted to stock space, and special workrooms were added for the carpet fitters of that time. "Upon this whole, this may safely be pronounced the most extensive, as it is most enterprising and successful dry goods house in the state, outside of Boston."[3]

Chapter 4
A Greater Presence

The business of Denholm and McKay had more than doubled since its opening in 1882 in the Clark Building, and more than six times as many dry goods were being sold per year. Irving Swan Brown (brother of Abel Swan), who had been brought on board as vice-president, sold his shares to his brother Luther in 1906, making Luther president and general manager. Other board members were G.E. Newkirk as vice-president and Irving Swan Brown and Frank Krim as treasury members. Luther C. Brown was active in the Worcester community and well admired. He served on many boards and was a member of the Worcester Club, the Tatnuck Country Club and the Hermitage Country Club. Being a part of society would further his relationship with the consumer and establish him as a community leader while in the end helping the business to flourish.

With the newly formed team in place, the business of servicing the clients and helping the employees started taking place, and the company was poised for its next period of growth. The Denholm Relief Fund was started by the employees of the company and would guarantee a payout in the event of sickness, disability or death. Should the employee leave the company, the insurance was forfeited. More employee services were added, such as an on-site nurse, an employee cafeteria and an employee say in the daily business practices. (Some of these services were developed by the associates and some had been in place in other retailers throughout the country, such as Filene's in Boston.) Management knew the employees were vital to allowing the business to grow and prosper. It was the associates who worked the closest with the customers and knew their wants and needs. With so many new businesses in the area, it was vital to keep the employees satisfied to maintain their loyalty.

INTERIOR CHANGES

Several interior modifications had taken place over the years, including the addition of the annex, which was built to help expand the footprint of the building. In 1916, a more ambitious renovation took place. The company already owned the building and property it was on, so any expansion could be done with greater ease. The company hired the firm of Frost and Chamberlain to do the exterior work and Tussig and Flesch for interior improvements. A total of $500,000 was poured into the renovations, and the plans were announced to the public. Most of the funding was supplied by banks, and the rest of the capital was provided from the Syndicated Trading Company.

The original square footage was at 150,000, and the new renovations would expand the store to 250,000. The most notable change would be an expansion to the original annex. Removal of the existing foot bridge to High Street and widening of the connection from the old structure to the newly built one made for a seamless transition. Staircases were widened again, and three more were added to give greater access to the basement region. The blueprints also called for an addition of a sixth floor, as the company owned the air rights to the building. The new level was made possible with the addition of structural reinforcements, which were anchored into the basement and first floors to support the added weight. Eight new state-of-the-art, wrought-iron-encased plunger elevators were installed to transport customers to all six levels. The main floor was completely renovated in the spirit of the Bon Marche Company based in Seattle. Dark oak bead board trimmed the walls and passageways, while large custom wall units were installed to give greater hanging capacity. Overhead pendant lights were replaced by larger milk glass fixtures able to illuminate the floor more evenly and be more pleasing to the eye.

Rearrangement of departments allowed for men's furnishings and clothing to be relocated to the first floor, as well as an expanded shoe department that could service 150 customers at any given time. The rest of the main floor was composed of notions, lace and cloth, silver and leather goods, jewelry, books and stationery, as well as various smaller-scaled departments. The second floor housed silk and dress goods, white goods, millinery, underwear and housedresses, corsets and infant wear. The third floor was expanded and primarily devoted to daytime dressing, including misses and children's suits and dresses, shirtwaists and woolen items. A new fur salon was added to the front of the floor and included full-length furs and accessories. A custom workroom was added to work on made-to-order suits and cloaks. The fourth floor now contained china, bric-a-brac, furniture and lamps, as well as various sporting goods. The marking and counting rooms, as well as the executive offices, were moved to the fifth floor, as well as mattresses and linens. The addition of the sixth floor made room for a newly built restaurant for customers, as well as a cafeteria that solely fed employees. New plumbing made it possible to relocate the public and private toilets to the sixth floor, as well as separate men's and women's waiting rooms.

Other interior improvements would be made to offer "the greatest facilities for displaying and handling goods in every department."[4] The main façade of the building was enhanced by a new, grander entrance, which was made wider than previously built. This was flanked by heavy steel doors more substantial in weight and design and helped to give the building a more "stately" appeal. New transom windows installed both front and rear allowed for cooling during the warmer summer months and gave much-needed airflow to the interior departments at no cost. The show window displays were completely refurbished and enlarged. New single-pane glass ornamented with iron details gave a cleaner appearance to the main focus of the store. All eight show windows were now under newly installed hunter green awnings that shielded the customer from the sun and inclement weather. These awnings also helped to reduce sun damage to clothing and other items being showcased, as well as the wax mannequins that would have melted unless kept at a constant temperature and away from direct sunlight. Throughout the building process, fireproof materials were used whenever possible. The installation of a modern sprinkler system was fed throughout the store and window displays to further protect the structure and its contents. Additional fireproof doors were added to the third floor and were designed to close easily and contain any flames should the respective departments be at risk. In a few years, these new additions to the safety of the building would be put to the test.

In 1916, the Denholm and McKay Company relied primarily on cash sales. Credit was given to top-tier customers who spent the most or had valuable ties to the community. The issue management was facing was that the debt on credit was adding up and depleting the margins of the company. A solution needed to be found to help the store maintain its profits while still granting credit. James Wilson made a suggestion to the senior team members. Wilson, who was a founding member of the National Retail Credit Association, was also the director, secretary and treasure of the Denholm and McKay Realty Company. Wilson proposed adding fees or fines to customers who were delinquent on their payment. He also proposed adding monthly billing cycles in which finance charges could be applied to the outstanding balance on the account. If all credit was paid off, the customer would have no fines. The new finance charges were applauded and implemented by the retail community, but customers were offended. Nonetheless, the new change to credit was adapted and helped the company by utilizing the charges or late fees to add to the bottom line.

As a modern convenience to the customers, modern pneumatic tubes or carriers were added throughout the store. Back then, there were no cash registers to accept payment on the selling floor. All transactions were sent downstairs to the credit department. Oftentimes there were floor runners who would take the cash for payment and run it down the stairs, collect the change if needed and bring it back up to the customer. With the addition of the new tubing system, which ran on a vacuum pressure operated by the electrical plant in the rear of the building, small cartridges with an opening for the payment were inserted into the large tubing system, and suction would carry them to the credit department.

This allowed for a quicker transaction for the customer and also allowed for more ventilation of the sales floor by the added air it provided.

In 1918, a change in the management team brought in some new talent to the store, and new directors were named. They consisted of John E. White, who was the president of the Worcester Bank and Trust Company; Joseph O. Proctor Jr., a businessman based in Boston; Henry Wolf of New York, who was the treasurer of the Syndicate Trading Company; and Frank Krim, who was elected as director to succeed Ernest Newkirk, who resigned. John E. White was made president, and James Wilson remained as treasurer. On March 12, 1918, the Denholm and McKay Realty Trust was formed to maintain control over the purchase of the land and the buildings that housed the company.

KNOWLES FIRE

On January 19, 1921, the Denholm and McKay Company would suffer its first losses. About 3:00 a.m., a great fire broke out two doors down at the Knowles Building on the corner of Main and Chatham Streets. The structure was an older office building made of brick and wood, with retail on the first and part of the second floor. S.S Kresge was the main tenant, occupying most of the first floor and part of the second. A janitor for the S. Marcus Company (a local furrier with space in the building) was in the process of cleaning the store when he observed flames coming up the central elevator shaft. He immediately rang the bells to alert the fire department. Several factors led to the rapid spread of the fire. The Knowles Building had a brick façade composed of large plate-glass windows, which were stationary. The interior design of the building was configured with brick walls around the perimeter and wood walls all throughout the interior, allowing for a larger central configuration. Several flammable materials had been used throughout construction of the building, including beaver wood and various veneers; both of these materials had dried out over the years. An antiquated sprinkler system was in place but had not been maintained in the previous ten years and only serviced the basement area and closets. The brick interior walls did not reach the top floor, and unprotected openings at the wood roof acted like a flue for the flames to spread.

When firefighters arrived, burning embers had gone airborne, and several local buildings were at risk. Next door to the Knowles Building was the company of Richard Healy. Richard Healy was an upscale store selling high-end women's furs and clothing. The Healy Building had two firewalls, both sixteen inches thick, on either side. One wall was next to the Knowles Building, and the opposite side was abutting the Denholm and McKay store. These firewalls helped to protect the Healy Company from the impending flames, and only minor smoke damage occurred.

With the winds picking up, embers made their way onto the sixth floor of the Denholm and McKay Building. Several firefighters made their way up to the roof and started throwing water on the flames to save the building. The inner fire doors were used for the first time and closed off the interior of the store to help contain any fire that might occur. At the same time, sprinkler heads went off in the south side of the building near the elevator shafts. The sprinklers helped to fend off the flames, but water damage occurred on all six floors, including the basement.

The fire continued throughout the day, as neighboring buildings were susceptible to the airborne flames that traveled down Main Street. At the end of this horrifying experience, the downtown area was a ghost town. Most of the buildings that did suffer damage were encased in ice from the freezing temperatures and the heavy use of water used to douse the flames.

The following day, the Denholm and McKay Company remained closed as cleanup of the water-damaged areas was surveyed and any merchandise that was ruined was swiftly removed from the selling floor. Insurers were at the building and calculated the total loss at $23,549,[5] a small price to pay considering the state of the rest of the downtown structures.

Upon further investigation, firefighters believed that a smoking cigarette left unattended on the fifth floor of the Knowles Building was the cause of the fire, but no one was ever charged in the event. With the great fire behind them, the city of Worcester started the process of rebuilding its future. New structures went up with stricter fire codes and updated sprinkler systems. The Knowles Building was leveled, and a new structure was planned to fill its space.

Chapter 5
Krim's Early Years

During a 1920s reorganization of the company, Frank Krim was promoted to the position of vice-president and general manager of the Denholm and McKay store and now had a financial interest in the company after becoming a partial owner. He, along with Henry Wolf from the Syndicated Trading Company and a silent partner, owned the building and a controlling interest in the shares. Krim, who entered the company in 1906 as a board member, was born in Boston and had his first job at the age of fourteen with the Carey-Fulton Company. His next job led him to the William Filenes and Sons Company in Boston. Filene's was one of the largest department stores in the country and was innovative in its contributions to associate and customer practices that had been implemented over its early years. Krim took a position as a buyer of misses and children's clothing and eventually held reign over the top ten departments, as well as overseeing junior buyers. He was soon promoted to merchandise manager, overseeing the buying team and department managers. Krim, who relocated to the area, had a growing family with his wife, Ida. Married in 1896, they had three children: Charles Fredrick, born in August 1897, eventually grew up and attended Phillips Academy and went on to be a buyer for the women's ready-to-wear departments at the Denholm and McKay Company; Claire Gertrude was born in 1899 and became a graduate of the Manhanttanville Academy, leaving in 1917; and the youngest daughter, Elizabeth Wood, born on September

30, 1910, would continue into adulthood to have connections to the Denholm and McKay Company after her father's death.

Krim was very knowledgeable of the dry goods trade and held many conferences for members of the retail community, as well as with his direct competition. These meetings were often held in the restaurant on the sixth floor. Topics of conversation included how to drive sales through stronger advertising efforts or how to develop working relationships with vendors. Krim was widely respected in the retail community and often traveled to other states to give lectures to other retailers such as Wanamaker's in Philadelphia or Gladdings in Rhode Island. He was a well-dressed man with a distinguished air about him. His gray hair and moustache added to his worldly appeal, and his eloquent way of speaking drew crowds. He was very in touch with the Worcester community and joined several local organizations, such as the Worcester Country Club, the Rotary Club and the chamber of commerce.

His passion for the business and the store itself helped to foster a greater appreciation among the employees. He was actively involved in all aspects of the store and paid great attention to the manner in which the product was being merchandised. Departments such as men's furnishings and clothing were growing in volume yearly, and Krim played an active role in having the proper assortments available at any given time. In 1922, he held a conference with the Retail Trade on the importance of having adequate floor space devoted to the specific needs of the male consumer. Another lecture was given on the importance of the Stoutwear merchandise assortment and placement of larger-size clothing for women. Krim approached a board of retailers alongside A. Grube of the A Grube Company based in Logansport, Indiana. The two talked about the importance of this sector of the market, as it was composed of 40 percent of the female customers. They lectured about giving the merchandise specific areas of its own where it would not be mixed in with misses-sized merchandise. They also advised dealing directly with the manufacturers to have new silhouettes produced that would flatter the figure while remaining comfortable in their sizing. The pair offered suggestions for copy to be placed in window displays alongside larger-scale bust forms to be provided by the manufacturers. "The volume that this department can bring to a store total is

Frank A. Krim.

immeasurable,"[6] claimed Krim.

On August 20, 1923, after returning from a speaking engagement in Europe, a "Welcome Home" dinner was arranged for Mr. Krim and his wife and at the Hotel Warren in Worcester. The engagement was held by the executives and buyers for the store as a thank-you for his endless hard work in traveling and promoting the business. The banquet featured iced Montreal melon, baby roasted squab chicken and new peas with mint, among other garnishes, and was finished off with a dessert of baked Alaska. Krim was touched by the employees' thoughtfulness and gave a lengthy speech about the future of the company and the important role that each individual played in the success of the store. As a token of his appreciation, he, along with the executives of the store, started yearly outings for the associates. All-day sporting events consisting of swimming, baseball and racing contests held on the shores of Lake Quaboag in Brookfield, Massachusetts. After the games were over, a large formal dinner with an awards ceremony would be held to recognize associates with twenty-five years of dedication to the company. Large floral bouquets would be handed out, along with twenty-five dollars in cash to each recipient, as a gesture of gratitude.

Besides giving lectures to other retailers, Krim enjoyed hearing what the store's associates had to say and listened intently. At the time, the advertising manager, Richard Toomey, approached him about starting a paper specifically targeted to the employees of the store. Toomey, who was nationally known for his contributions to the advertising world, joined the Denholm and McKay Company in 1917. Previously, he had held various positions with Forbes and Wallace, as well as R.H. Whites in Boston. The paper that Toomey would create would be used solely for internal purposes and would be written by the associates for the associates. Krim liked the idea and thought it would be a good vehicle to enhance morale at the store. Before anything would go to press, the management team would approach the employees to get their feedback. All levels of employees were spoken to, including buyers, clerks and staff working behind the scenes. Other stores such as Forbes and Wallace, as well as Filene's, already had internal papers, and the reading proved to be quite popular with the staff. After the project was approved by the associates, a formal editor and full staff of officers was soon in place. A contest for a name was started, with a five-dollar reward for the winner. After many submissions, the name *The Tattler* won the majority vote of the employees. In this publication, associates could write about any issues within the store, a new book that they read or a favorite recipe. Krim enjoyed reading the papers and often showed them to his various business colleagues.

During his daily floor walks through the store, he loved to interact with the associates and ask what was selling or not selling, which customers had been in lately or if there were any issues in the store that needed to be addressed. His charismatic personality made him very easy to approach, and the staff of the store would anticipate his arrival to their respective departments. Both customers and employees found his passion for public speaking intoxicating, and conversations would often last longer than intended. Krim and Toomey partnered with other retailers in the city of Worcester and often would have lunchtime meetings with the various senior management related to those stores. The topics of conversation would consist of business trends, buying issues and local events.

Denholm and McKay was not the only retailer in Worcester. Barnard, Putnam and Sumner had been established earlier, and there was C.T. Sherer on Front Street, as well as the John C. MacInnes store on Main Street. Mr. MacInnes started his business as a jobber of wholesale goods to other retailers. Soon he decided to forego being in that sector of the market and chose to open up his own store. The new retail store consisted of hosiery and underwear, cloaks and suits and various dry goods. With its growing business, MacInnes's soon expanded its floor space and offerings. Much like William A. Denholm, John MacInnes was a native of Scotland and came to Worcester to continue his career.

Fashion at that time was undergoing a radical change. Simple sheath dresses were replacing the heavier layered look of the Victorians. With their straight, effortless design, they eliminated the need for corsetry, which had been a major selling department in years past. Hair was now bobbed and often straightened into chin-length blunt cuts. Large hats often adorned with feathers, tulle and ribbons now adapted to simple cloche designs that sat snugly on the wearer's head. Department stores like Denholm and McKay started to introduce dress and clothing departments that offered ready-made garments. The high-end customer could still have her suits and dresses made by hand in the alterations department, but the average middle-class shopper couldn't afford those steep prices. Ready-made garments had been widely produced both locally and abroad and gave the customers more choices for their wardrobes. The fabric and trimmings department that previously had anchored the main floor was now moved to the second floor, as only lower-income shoppers were still producing their own wardrobes. With the rise of women's hemlines, more attention was being placed on the leg. Simple dresses or knee-length skirts made out of wool or silk were often paired with silk or rayon spun hosiery with French seams and reinforced heels.

The changes in fashion played a major role in how the store was mapped out. Hosiery was now given a more prominent location on the first floor alongside the accessories department, which housed scarves and gloves. Costume jewelry, with its bolder approach to design and new materials such as resin (often known as Bakelite), demanded more case line space among the jewelry departments of the day. Denholm and McKay devoted an additional eight cases to the growing trend. The appeal of the movies being made in Hollywood featured glamorous stars with their plucked eyebrows, smoky eye makeup and small, red, pursed lips. Consumers wanted to look like their film idols, and cosmetic lines started to be introduced on a larger level. Denholm and McKay formed a separate department solely devoted to cosmetics and creams. Case lines were installed, and individual items' numbers were added to track sales. Specially placed associates were educated and trained to give the customer more assistance and guidance with their makeup selections.

The inner workings of the Denholm and McKay Company needed to change and adapt to the rapidly growing field of merchandise it was now carrying. Along with the fashion changes, there were larger electric appliances being offered. Washing machines, fans and radios needed more floor space alongside the existing furniture and appliance departments. To promote these goods, the advertising department, which was in house, needed to expand. Not only did it still have to write the newspaper ads, but it was also now producing local radio spots to alert customers of new items or special events within the store. The display department, headed up by William Farrington, also needed to expand, as more attention was being paid to the look and feel of the store. The window displays, which in previous years had been chock full of merchandise often fanned out or displayed in bulk, were now simplified and edited to highlight certain trends or new inventions. The displays along Main Street took on a more lavish feeling. Residential settings showcasing furniture groupings were shown with the appropriate wall coverings, rugs and decoratives that would coordinate. The fashion windows now highlighted a few mannequins completely accessorized from head to toe with the flapper look. These wax figures were often poised in front of simple deco screens or palm trees in oriental fish pots. Special in-store promotions that tied into advertising were often given window exposure. A new group of furs could be displayed in front of papier-mâché icebergs with glittering details and snowy ice caps with a copy of the weekly ad placed alongside the coordinating accessories. Interior displays were also introduced on a more formal level. Mannequins placed around the women's departments showed the customer the proper ways to wear the new looks and styles, complete with human hair wigs and the appropriate accessories. Men's bust forms were often rigged on the first floor, complete with an assortment of shirts and ties that coordinated with the item being advertised.

Denholm and McKay regarded newspaper advertising as most beneficial to promoting in-store events and sales. The *Worcester Telegram* was the largest target, as it reached the most people in the central Massachusetts area. Ads for white sales, home furnishings and clothing were often illustrated by the on-site advertising department, and all copy was written in house under Toomey's direction. One such ad in June 1924 read, "You will appreciate NOW perhaps more than at any time of the year the spaciousness of Denholm & McKay's great floors which extend from to High Street down to Main. With the broad aisles and the perfect ventilation and lighting systems and the many other conveniences typical of the better store." Advertising and mailings were the primary

Main Street, circa 1920s. *Left to right*: S.S. Kresge, Richard Healy Company and Denholm and McKay Company.

Filene's Department store, 531 Main Street. *Courtesy of the Boston Public Library.*

way to reach the customers at the time. Well-written and often highly illustrated ads featuring stylized drawings of women in flapper dresses, men in three-piece suits fully accessorized with ties and collar bars or newly invented appliances graced multiple pages of the *Telegram and Gazette*. With the change in men's and women's fashions, advertising was vital to get the message of the store to the masses.

By the late 1920s, a new store would enter the retail center of Worcester and add another name to the list. On March 1928, William Filene's and Sons took over a former space occupied by the Laskey Company. The building was erected after the 1921 fire took down the existing one that stood there. The new building located at 531 Main Street consisted of a limestone and green marble façade. Oversized windows with beautifully appointed details allowed plenty of sunlight to flood the interior. The structure was three floors high and was filled primarily with women's and children's clothing.

At the opening, menswear was not incorporated, but it would be added at a later date when the building was expanded. A huge driving force of the store was its bargain basement. Long a Boston institution, the basement offered exceptional goods sold below retail prices. Often filled with overstock from other manufacturers, the Filene's Company could offer deeper discounts than other retailers and often would sell its goods with a minimal margin. Filene's already had stores in Boston, Wellesley, Providence and Portland, but the Worcester store would be its second largest in operation. Employing one hundred associates (most were retained from the Laskey Company), they were trained under the high standards of selling and service that were implemented throughout the company.

The Denholm and McKay Company welcomed the addition of supplementary retailers, as the consumer base was growing. In 1920, the population in Worcester had risen to 195,311, up from 41,105 in 1870. Several smaller chain stores had begun to open on Main Street selling more specialized categories of merchandise, mostly in the form of dress shops or children's clothing. The addition of these stores only strengthened the downtown shopping district, and Denholm and McKay had already established a fine reputation as the leader in the area. The company never tried to compete on levels at which it was not established. Selling off-price goods was not its market. A continued focus on customer service and quality merchandise was what it spoke to.

At that time, most goods were still being paid for in cash, and credit was given to select customers whose buying power increased yearly. In early 1929, James Wilson (credit manager) gave a speech to a group of industry men in Providence, Rhode Island, on the "moral risk in business." Wilson stated that it was in a department store's best interest to fairly give credit to worthy customers. Stores like Denholm and McKay could not extend themselves financially without a proven record that a customer could pay them back. Stricter guidelines needed to be implemented to screen the applicant's financial history.

Within a few months, the October stock market crash in 1929 would force Denholm and McKay and the entire country to reevaluate the way they were doing business.

Chapter 6
A Change in Business Practices

The stock market crash had major impacts on all sectors of life. Many people lost life savings as banks folded under massive withdrawal of funds by patrons and shareholders. The reality of this tragedy took hold in the form of long unemployment lines, foreclosures on housing and a drop in consumer spending. Fortunately, the city of Worcester was still a vital center for manufacturing. Employment dropped off, but it was not as severe as in other areas of the country.

Given the current state of the nation, the Denholm and McKay Company was forced to look at the business in a new light. The 1920s had been prosperous years, with new designs in fashions and home furnishings leading the business. The 1930s would prove to be a more somber approach to retailing. Women's fashions of the '20s, with their slim silhouette and boyish figure, removed the need for fitted undergarments. The 1930s silhouette was more feminine, with a return to the waistline and the need for proper underpinnings. Brassieres were now needed to achieve the current movement in fashion. A formal foundations department was added to the second floor, with a greater offering of goods including bras, girdles and slips. Most of these items were embellished with lace details, which brought a more feminine approach to dressing. While sales in ladies' departments were remaining strong, sales in men's suiting had dropped off. A total analysis of the business was needed to continue to operate in the black.

John Hughes, merchandise manager for Denholm and McKay, held a conference with other leaders in the retail market to discuss the "Risk of Cheapness" in stores during that timeframe. The symposium was held at the Hotel Pennsylvania, where various discussions revolved around the ability to maintain quality merchandise during a time of consumer recession. Hughes maintained that Denholm and McKay would never sell goods that were below its standards. Too many merchants were opting to sell cheap goods at lower price points just to make a sale. Mr. Hughes added that many stores were eliminating higher-price-point goods and, in return, replacing them with lower-quality items that eroded the store's image. "Quality must be good," he said. "People cannot afford to buy poor or uncertain merchandise."[7] The association went on to discuss how important it was not to overly advertise or display cheap, lower price points in hopes of a sale. Higher ticket sales and trading up of items could be achieved, should the consumer be made not to feel guilty for spending more for excellence. Departments were carefully observed to track sales and allocate proper floor space and window exposure to more rapidly selling items. Denholm and McKay continued business in the early 1930s with only a modest drop in business due to its continued focus on maintaining healthy margins and not succumbing to what other retailers were dictating.

The interior of the store had evolved over the years. Modifications were continually being made to service and display the merchandise in the most up-to-date setting. The oak bead board that once adorned the main floor was now being removed, and simple plaster walls with applied molding took its place. In an effort to boost business with the male customer, the men's furnishings and clothing department on the first floor was remodeled to fashion a more streamlined look. Large wall units were installed to house more suiting alongside free-standing bunkers that displayed men's trousers. A seating area was arranged with leather and chrome chairs and silver standing ashtrays, and the daily papers were displayed on reading sticks made out of bamboo with silver handles. Customers could relax and read the latest news, smoke a cigar or converse with other patrons. The upper floors were also updated with new color schemes of light green and beige paint on the furniture floor, as well as pale blue used in the children's areas. The women's evening dresses department was also modernized with a soft pink and green color palette, and new wall fixtures were added to highlight the various satin bias-cut gowns that were in fashion at the time.

In 1936, Denholm and McKay celebrated its sixty-fifth birthday with full-page ads heralding the event. The focus of this occasion was to highlight the modernity of the store, as well as the offering of the latest fashions. In preparation for the event, management from each department attended "fashion clinics" at the nation's leading merchandise marts focusing on the latest trends in women's clothing and millinery, as well as the latest styles in men's and home furnishings. Manufacturers produced exclusive merchandise for the sale during the event in appreciation for the past business they had obtained. The associates of the store were required to attend regular classes in merchandising and customer service that were conducted by the store's internal educational department. A new fleet of forest green delivery trucks with the Denholm and McKay logo freshly painted in white was added to transport customer purchases home for them. "The newest spring styles in apparel and furniture have been stocked, in keeping with the progressive keynotes of the sale… Time and expenses have not been spared…A few hours after a new style have proved successful in the metropolitan centers of the nation. The purchasing agents at Denholm's have all of the details on it."[8] A lot of hard work went into the celebration. The store was climbing out of the early 1930s, when sales were more modest. The year 1935 was the most profitable on record, and the goal was to surpass that year and maintain a healthy margin. Frank Krim addressed the shareholders of the company at their annual meeting and expressed his enthusiasm for the current business trend and his belief that the business would prosper through the fall. Reelection of the board also took place with Krim as president, James A. Swan as vice-president, Henry Wolf as treasurer and William E. Darling as assistant treasurer and clerk.

Along with the sixty-fifth anniversary, Denholm and McKay continued to use events as a way to drive more traffic into the store. Each Christmas season, shoppers could find their way up to the furniture department on the fourth floor, where a section was devoted to Christmas decorations, cards and wrapping paper. The center of the department was transformed into a winter wonderland with large oversized reindeer, glittering Christmas decorations and, most of all, Santa. Little boys and girls would wait patiently in line for their turn to tell Santa what they wanted for the holiday. To keep the children occupied while waiting, custom coloring books were handed out. The stories would consist of such holiday favorites as *The Night before Christmas* or *Rudolph, the Red-Nosed Reindeer*. Large train sets were displayed on tables in conjunction with other toys suitable for young boys, and little girls could marvel at the newest baby doll or stuffed animals nestled within the glass display cases. The exterior of the store also received a festive treatment with a large traditional tree and three-story candles all made out of lights that illuminated Main Street. To many, it would be the start of a family tradition to go to Denholm and McKay and visit with Santa or to listen to the Denholm Choir singing Christmas carols being broadcast over the local radio station WTAG.

Besides the holidays, the store created various in-store events during slow selling months as a way to lure in shoppers. One such promotion was the Cutest Baby event, which was held in the children's department on the third floor. Hundreds of shoppers brought their newborns into the store and paraded them around in front of a panel of judges. Nestled inside polished prams, the infants were dressed up in their finest attire, unaware of the contest in which they were involved. The panel of adjudicators consisted of the store executives and manufacturers like Carters, which supplied clothing to the store. When the chosen baby was named, the local press would be on hand to take the inaugural photo and announce the winner in print. Other smaller-scale events included fashion clinics on the women's third-floor dress department, where a team of stylists were assembled to inform the consumer on current fashion, hair and makeup trends that were popularized during the 1930s. These stylists consisted of beauticians from the beauty salon, representatives with the cosmetic lines and editors from national fashion magazines. On some occasions, a chosen customer was handpicked out of the crowd to receive a full makeover, complete with new accessories and an outfit, courtesy of the store.

In 1935, silent film star Colleen Moore exhibited her ongoing passion with a fairy castle dollhouse she had built with the assistance of more than seven hundred individuals who had lent their expertise, including Hollywood lighting specialists, Beverly Hills jewelers and Chinese jade craftsmen. The total size of the childlike fairy castle was eight feet, seven inches by eight feet, two inches by seven feet, seven inches. It was retrofitted with more than two thousand miniatures, including furniture, chandeliers and a fully manicured garden. The cost to erect such a detailed reproduction totaled more than $500,000. Her castle was transformed by the Great Depression into a passion for helping children. She organized a national tour of the fairy castle to raise money for children's charities. Having been showcased in Bloomingdale's and Macy's New York, the next leg of the journey brought the tour to Denholm and McKay. Shoppers could pay an entrance fee of $1 and view the lavishly decorated dream house and meet the star during a private cocktail reception held in her honor. Even though times were tough financially for the local customers, the store conveyed a glimpse of hope that brighter days were ahead.

An Engagement

In 1938, Elizabeth Krim (Frank Krim's daughter) became engaged to Russell Corsini. The two were avid tennis players who met while playing at a mixed couple's tournament in Worcester. Corsini was a graduate of Worcester Polytechnic Institute in 1931 and received his master's degree in chemistry in 1933. He taught at Commerce High and North High School and was a gifted pianist who enjoyed playing classical and popular pieces. Corsini came on board as a floorwalker in the housewares department, working part time until he was promoted to merchandising manager within a few years. Russell Corsini had long been interested in retail and had excelled at the miscellaneous tasks and positions that he had become familiar with. His new position would allow for further growth within the company, as well as an invested interest in the business.

Frank Krim was now formally assembling a new management team that could carry the store through the end of the Depression and into the future.

Chapter 7

The War Years

With the Depression just a few years back, Denholm and McKay was moving into the new decade with expansion and modernization on its mind. The store was marking its sixty-ninth anniversary in 1940, and several more improvements had been made under the control of Krim. "In a sense," he stated, "we never stop building, improving, or modernizing. Not a day goes by year in and year out, but that finds some new refinement in the nearly eight acres of floor space occupied by our store."[9] The interior updates included a refurbishing of the women's shoe salon on the first floor, where beige linen was applied on the walls to give a soft and textural feeling, while coral-colored accents punctuated the display tables and newly installed soffits hid the fluorescent lighting. Espresso brown and cream zebra prints were used as upholstery for the customer seating, which made the department one of the most beautiful and successful shoe salons in the East. The entire south half of the second floor, which housed bedding, towels and yard goods, had custom-built fixtures installed, with small vignettes inserted on each end to display coordinating items to their full advantage. Behind all the display beds stood newly erected walls with backlit windows showing the appropriate window fashions to complement the room. On the fourth floor, a group of eleven rooms named the Pendleton Shops was installed and decorated by a group of interior designers. These rooms featured furniture, draperies, rugs and ornamental accessories that complemented the differing styles of each space. Interior designers were now employed in store to service the customer in coordinating appropriate looks based on the current trends in home decor. The former beauty salon and men's barbershop, where little boys would sit on rocking wooden horses while getting a haircut, was now closed, and a new beauty salon geared solely to women was installed on the sixth floor. It offered hairdressings, facials, manicures and pedicures, all within a modern "white on white" environment with sleek chrome and glass partitions.

Throughout the entire store, modern fluorescent lighting was added to walls and ceilings to even out any shadows produced by the former incandescent fixtures and create a more modern, well-lit interior. All six floors had now been updated with fresh paint, wall treatments and lighting, making for a more contemporary environment to shop in. The exterior of the building also received a minor update by replacing the former hunter green awnings with new ones in emerald green, terra cotta and cream stripes. To further commemorate the anniversary, the shopping bags, which were a natural brown with black Denholm and McKay script emblazoned across the front, were changed out for simple white bags with an art deco–inspired "DM" monogrammed in the center and "Denholm and McKay The Boston Store" wrapping the initials in a circular formation. Management wanted to attract the younger generation to start shopping in the store, and new and modern signage would complement its image as a fashion leader. Most of the younger generations at this time now referred to the store as simply Denholms, abandoning the former "Boston Store" term as a relic of days gone by. The executives started to hold focus groups of younger customers and ask them precisely what they were looking for in a shopping environment. Most commentary was taken quite seriously, and every effort to implement new and noteworthy ideas was made possible.

Constant analysis of the business was a must, as fashions and wartime rations were changing what the store would sell and offer to its customers. John Hughes, who was carrying out his final year as merchandise manager of Denholms, gave a lecture in the Hotel Pennsylvania on the importance of analyzing departments that operated in the red. He stated that every observance should be made to focus on the underperforming departments and that profits were not impossible given proper exposure and attention. Hughes also advised introducing more cost-friendly dress departments to stores, as they had better margins and a faster sell through, which would offset the higher-priced goods being sold in the better dress departments.[10]

By December of the same year, Frank A. Krim was reelected president of Denholm and McKay at the annual stockholders' meeting in New

York. Other officers of the department store reelected were James A Swan, vice-president; Henry Wolf, treasurer; and William Daring, assistant treasurer and clerk. Harry F. Wolf (Henry's younger son) was elected as a director, along with Anthony Adrian and James Strong. The Denholm and McKay Realty Company continued to be headed up by Adrian, with James Wilson as treasurer and clerk.[11] Russell Corsini was now promoted to merchandise manager overseeing all areas of the store until a replacement could be found for John Hughes's areas of responsibility. Corsini's duties included maintaining a healthy margin, controlling expenses and managing and overseeing the buyers for each department, in addition to various merchandising tasks. The executive team was in position, but it would be short-lived, as many changes were on the horizon.

By 1943, World War II was in full swing, and rations of tin, silk and fabric were making for changes within the organization. Some employees of the store (mostly men) were sent abroad to fight, and women filled their positions. Like many stores of the days, Denholms wanted to help the country in any way possible. War bonds were advertised in the display windows on Main Street alongside the patriotically dressed mannequins, as well as being sold on the first floor by government personnel. Departments such as hosiery and lingerie were scaled down as rations on rayon and silk made production of those items nonexistent. Fortunately, women's accessories and millinery would offset the decline in sales, and those departments were given more floor space and advertising dollars to promote. With the rations on fabric in place, women's clothing changed to a more structured and boxy silhouette, with slim pencil skirts and large padded shoulders using as little as three to four yards of fabric per garment. A new ladies' suit section was added to the third floor adjacent to the north bank of elevators. Large, free-standing wall units made out of maple and glass housed the garments, while free-standing tables displayed coordinating hats and gloves perfect for any attire. A formal seating arrangement of four tightly structured chairs anchored the room, and stylized mannequins showcased the most up-to-date trends being presented. Here women could shop for suiting and blouses appropriate for their new jobs in the workplace, all within a relaxing environment.

In August of that same year, Henry Wolf passed away unexpectedly at the age of seventy-three due to a stroke. Besides being a treasurer for Denholm and McKay, Wolf had been on the executive board at the Novelty Handkerchief Company based in New York. Formerly he had been president of Almay stores, which was based out of Montreal. He left behind his wife, Crescentia, and his two sons, Harry and Paul. Within a few years, Harry Wolf would enter the Worcester store and take Denholms into the next decade.[12] Before that transition would take place, darker days would lie ahead.

In the summer of 1945, a young boy named Edward Hakenson was shopping with his mother at the store. The two separated while she was buying supplies, and young Edward went off exploring on his own. He managed to slip out the second-floor rear entrance through the mailroom and made his way down into Chase Court (which was the alley that ran under the store between the annex and original building). The young boy made his way into the freight elevator used by the store by climbing through an opening above the wooden door used to secure the elevator. The youngster fell down a floor and landed on top of the elevator as it was stationed on the basement level. An associate on an upper floor, unaware of what had happened, rang for the elevator, and little Edward was caught up in the cables that raised and lowered the machine. The young boy's cries rang out, and the engineer on duty quickly stopped the car from operating. When police and ambulances arrived, the little boy was lying still on top of the boxcar. Every attempt was made to save the young boy's life, but it was too late. The following day, the store was closed as police and investigators retraced his steps to see how this tragedy could have happened. In the following days, store executives attended the funeral of the youngster, and a moment of silence was held at Denholms as a remembrance. Stricter codes were enforced, and a steel double door was erected to ensure this kind of catastrophe would never happen again.

With the tragedies of the previous years still fresh in everyone's minds, the subsequent year would prove to be just as distressing. On July 8, 1946, Mr. and Mrs. Krim went to Maine to summer at a resort. The vacation was cut short, as a heart condition forced Krim to seek medical attention. The medical team that was assembled treated his condition, but on July 19, 1946, Frank A. Krim passed away at the age of seventy-eight. Local and national newspapers ran large-scale obituaries on the former retail legend. The lengthy articles written about him spanned his career and covered his many trips to Europe, where he combined business and pleasure. Krim was an avid art collector as well as a devout Catholic, and in 1942, he received the highest honor from the head of the Roman Catholic Church when he was made a Knight of Malta.[13] Store executives and associates mourned the passing of their leader at a Mass that they all attended, where they recognized his many achievements. A new search was on for a replacement who could lead Denholms on the level that Mr. Krim had delivered. Months would go by until the proper candidate could be found.

Chapter 8
A New Look

At the start of 1947, Harry Wolf was elected by the board of directors to succeed Krim as president and general manager of Denholms. Wolf, who was born in New York, attended Williams College and graduated in the class of 1929. He started his business career in finance with the Equitable Trust Company in New York and later worked with Chase National. From there, he went into management with the Novelty Handkerchief Company, based in Passaic, New Jersey. Harry Wolf was a national amateur squash champion who won eleven consecutive team matches, which ranked him as the number-one amateur player in the field. He was married to Alice Wolf, who was an avid sportswoman in her own right, playing golf as well as tennis. The two would amass hundreds of silver cup trophies for their winnings and enjoy the competition to the fullest. The couple lived in New Jersey and was raising a family of three boys—Harry Jr., John and Paul—and five daughters: Amy, Diana, Alice, Patricia and Pamela. With the acceptance of the position, Harry moved the family to the Worcester area and settled down in the town of Shrewsbury in a large majestic estate of Spanish style.

Mr. Wolf had been involved with the company as a director alongside his father for a few years and understood the retail business fully. His father's association with the firm helped to educate Harry about the Denholm and McKay history, as well as the advancements that had been made over the past decades. Harry, along with the board of directors, set

Harry Wolf.

forth to continue the legacy of the retail giant and implemented some concepts that had been previously discussed. The first such change was the addition of cash registers in every department. Up until this point, all transactions were sent to the central cash office by way of the pneumatic tube system. Having registers in every department would allow for the selling associates to have full control over each purchase and speed up the process for the customer. By 1948, more purchases were being made on store credit, with less being handled in cash. The new terminals would accept cash and have a separate hand machine to make imprints of the tin charge cards on carbon paper receipts. This whole process was designed to free up the cash office from the overwhelming number of transactions being handled on a daily basis. With the approval and funding in place by the board of directors, Denholms made the largest purchase of cash registers in the history of central Massachusetts.

Along with the revamping of the register system, a more in-depth renovation changed the look of Denholms forever. The war was over, and the servicemen and -women had returned home. The streets of Worcester were packed with people again in record numbers. The population of Worcester had risen to 203,486, the highest number of citizens on record. The former rations on fabric were now over, and Paris was setting the tone for what women would wear in the States. Christian Dior debuted his fall 1947 line that changed the silhouette completely. The slim pencil skirts and shoulder pads that had dominated wartime were now replaced with a more feminine profile consisting of soft, sloping shoulders, wasp waists and full, voluminous skirts that fell just above the ankle. Customers and the press heralded the "New Look," and within a year, it was introduced to the masses throughout the various design companies.

With the change in fashion as well as the introduction of more modern furniture and appliances on the marketplace, Denholms contemplated the exterior of the building and whether it projected the updated modern image that was in fashion at the time. With the approval of the board of directors, and capital invested by the Syndicated Trading Company, plans for an exterior renovation were put in place. The store sought out various architectural firms and chose the design firm of H.E. Davidson to draw up plans for the new façade. The new exterior would capture the simple, stylized designs popularized during the 1920s and '30s. H.E. Davidson was an established firm based out of Boston. The company designed for both residential and commercial spaces and won numerous awards for its simplistic approach to design. After months of study and meetings with Harry Wolf and the executives, a design was in place. The new plan would alleviate the myriad windows that covered the front of the building and focus the customers' attention down to the newly formed display windows.

Before demolition could begin, the company would suffer another loss. John Hughes, merchandise manager, passed away at the United States Veterans Hospital in Bedford. Hughes, who was an instrumental leader within the organization, was remembered for his hard work and involvement with the chamber of commerce. Several members of the retail trade, as well as the management team of Denholms, attended the funeral services, and a moment of silence was held at the store in remembrance of him.

With all the structural inspections completed, architectural blueprints were drawn up and evaluated by Harry Wolf. The drawings complemented the modern design movement that was appearing in all aspects of manufacturing, from furniture and appliances down to simple household gadgets. The building would be likened to various other department stores being built around the nation but was similar in design to the John Shillito Company in Cincinnati. The new façade bumped the building out by two feet to allow for an additional 10,000 square feet of stockrooms to be built on each of the five visible floors facing Main Street. In earlier years, sales clerks often had to leave the selling floor to go look for sizes or correct colors in remote stockrooms. The addition of space allocated to back stock would provide better customer service and allow associates greater ease when retrieving items. The external materials consisted of limestone slabs laid in a brick pattern on the higher floors, with narrow bands of windows set flush to the exterior. Each row of the upper windows was capped off with stainless steel bands reinforcing the horizontal design, and small fluted columns of the same material flanked each set of the opaque glass panes. The main floor and showcase windows took on a dramatic appearance as well. Black Belgian marble grounded the building, and the original three entrances were converted to two, allowing for more display space. At the time, the building had six display windows. The new design allowed for eight display windows on Main Street and for three to be added to the two new vestibules being planned. Customers would be greeted at the entrances by large Herculite glass doors with Lucite handles, nestled within the curved lines of the marble that capped off the display windows. But the biggest change added to the new front was a marquee that would extend over the sidewalk for the full 180 feet of the building. The marquee consisted of stainless steel with recessed lighting added to the underside and infrared lights at the entrances, which would keep shoppers warm while perusing the window displays. On top of the marquee, signage was installed in a deco font illuminated in neon stating "Denholm and McKay." The overall design was labeled as "Modernistic," which conveyed the interior image of the store to the sidewalk.

In early 1949, the wrought-iron railing that perched atop the building was removed to get ready for the major demolition project that would take place later that year. The local papers photographed the event, and the store issued a publicity release announcing its new plans to the public. The next work to be done was the removal of the small brick posts that anchored the railing, as well as the top of the grand central column that still bore the name of Jonas G. Clark. Large wooden scaffolding was erected over the sidewalk to prep for the removal of windows and the brick flourishes that covered the outer surface. Workmen chipped away at brick columns and window trim for months under large tarps that shielded the building to get the façade to an even level surface. New steel beams were inserted along the exterior to allow for the expansion of the new stockrooms, as well as to anchor the marquee that extended the building by ten feet. Crowds would watch daily to see the progress that was being made, and the local newspapers and radio stations captured the building's transformation.

The exterior was not the only modernizing project that was taking place with the structure. The interior of the store's first floor was changing shape as a large two- by twenty-five-foot dividing wall was removed to allow for a freer flow within the departments. Case lines, which in the past formed small squares or rectangles, were now reconfigured to create large, wide aisles that led to the elevators or the rear of the store. A new sweeping staircase done in wood and plaster with deco swirls at the end caps formed a new entrance to the basement level from the five-hundred-vestibule entrance, allowing another form of access to the lower level. The bridal salon on the third floor was also renovated in a new semicircular design, with a lit dome anchored in the ceiling of the rotunda. The walls of the shop were upholstered in a soft ivory silk, and gray duchess satin drapes concealed the fitting rooms strategically placed around the perimeter walls. A large mannequin platform with the latest bridal gown on display was the focal point of the shop. The overall space was softened with a seating arrangement of four chairs and a large glass coffee table placed in the center of the department. Millinery also relocated to a new home at the front of the store on the third floor. An additional five hundred square feet of selling space was added to expand the department. The perimeter walls displayed the latest hats in fashion, all perched on Lucite stands and stylized mannequin heads.

The center column and railing were removed in preparation for the façade change in 1949. *Courtesy of the* Worcester Telegram and Gazette.

Denholm and McKay during construction of the façade change. *From the collections of the Worcester Historical Museum, Worcester, Massachusetts.*

The interior floor space was furnished with modern tables made out of bleached wood and glass, with large mirrors affixed to each station where customers could sit down and get fitted for the appropriate hat.

With the exterior and interior renovations lasting over sixteen months, the final unveiling was held on Tuesday, April 17, 1951. Large, full-page spreads in the *Worcester Telegram* heralded the event. One ad included a letter from the mayor of Worcester, Andrew B. Holstrom, which stated:

> *Dear Mr. Wolf: As a Main Street neighbor, sharing with you an active interest in clean-cut techniques of administration, I extend to you and your company my warm commendation on your newly modernized store. The new exterior of your building, right across the street from my City Hall office window, is a fine one. I like this design very much. You are to be congratulated to, on the gains made in the interior. These constructive changes represent a very real community asset in the enhanced appearance of our downtown area and in the visible inspiration thus given for civil self-respect. As a company that has served for eighty one years, you have vitalized effectively the adage: "Whatever is worth doing at all—is worth doing well." Sincerely yours, A.B. Holstrom—Mayor.*[14]

The store held an official ribbon-cutting ceremony during a special dedication day that Wednesday. This was the first chance for shoppers to officially see the new Denholms façade in its completed form. A large crowd of shoppers showed up to gaze at the new storefront and modern display windows. The windows, which were manufactured by Pittsburgh Plate Glass Company, featured glazed and distortion-free glass that banished waves or imperfections during the manufacturing process. The large open panels were set in a ribbon sash made out of brushed aluminum with only a few vertical uprights to secure the glass. The newly formed window displays were more reserved than the ones of the previous years. New twenty-four-inch horizontal bands of simple beveled wood painted in a soft ivory wrapped each space, while new fixed circular lights illuminated the mannequins. The men's windows, which were now located on the left side of the building and interior vestibule, consisted of dark teak boards with a vertical notch done in a striae effect to differentiate that entrance to the store.

The displays within these spaces were the responsibility of Eric Hallback. Hallback, who was born in Worcester, was a former navy veteran who served in World War II, stationed in the submarine division. He came to Denholms with a degree in art from the Worcester Art Museum. Previously, he had been a window manager with the Filene's Company until being recruited to join the Denholms team. After a meeting with Harry Wolf where his portfolio and résumé were examined, he was named the display director for the store; responsibilities included all the store window displays and in-store events, as well as designing fixtures for various promotions. Hallback would become an enormous asset to the store, and his great eye for detail would become evident in the straightforward but exquisite vignettes that he would form.

The grand opening windows consisted of simple displays showcasing the latest trends in fashions tied in with the upcoming Easter holiday. Meticulously appointed female mannequins were dressed in rich navy

The 1951 women's opening windows, featuring Parisian-inspired fashions.

The 1951 opening window, featuring millinery fashions.

blue and dove gray coats and suits—all adorned with white kid gloves and portrait hats. The propping in each display consisted of hand-painted illustrations of the latest fashion silhouettes alongside an artist's palette. Each drawing was incorporated into the individual displays to highlight the trends of the season, whether it was dresses, hats or children's wear. With the show windows more integral to the storefront than in the past, a new streamlined look and feel was implemented. Subtle use of propping and mannequins helped to give a more modern, sophisticated air to the storefront.

Chapter 9
The Steadfast Years

In addition to the storefront modification, a new member would enter the Denholm and McKay executive team. Paul Wolf was Harry Wolf's younger brother. At a board meeting in New York, Paul was named a director with the company, as well as vice-president to Harry. Originally based out of New York, Paul eventually moved to the Worcester area to maintain a presence in the store. From a small office on the third floor, he oversaw the operational side of the store, with a strong focus on the shipping, receiving and marking rooms. Working alongside Russell Corsini and reporting to Harry Wolf, the team would help lead the store into its most prosperous decade.

In January 1952, a modern convenience was added to the Worcester store. Central air conditioning was rather new at the time, especially in large-scale stores such as Denholms. With the new small, narrow windows on the façade and stockrooms that now abutted them in place, ventilation of the store would be compromised. A major installation of cooling systems was placed on the roof that fed cold air to every part of the store through newly installed ductwork and discreet vents. Harry Wolf was so proud of the system that an ad ran in the Sunday paper stating, "Denholms is the first store in Worcester to be air-cooled. Come in and cool off while shopping our six floors of quality merchandise in a comfortable setting."

Besides the newly installed cooling system, another acquisition was about to take place. A two-and-a-half-story brick house owned by a doctor and his wife sat adjacent to the High Street receiving dock owned by Denholms. In an effort to obtain more space for future development, Harry Wolf and the Denholm and McKay Company purchased the house and the land that it sat on. In the beginning, the house was used as additional space for offices and a resting place for executives or traveling salesmen who frequented the store. In the early summer of 1953, the house became a safe haven for employees of the store. That year, in June, after a bout of hot and humid weather paired up against a cold front coming from the west, a tornado was formed in the Worcester area. Described as a "huge cone of dark smoke," the traveling twister made its way through the city and left massive destruction in its path. Some of the hardest-hit areas were Assumption College and the newly built Great Brook Valley apartments. A few employees and their families were renting spaces at the apartment complex and took cover as the storm hit. After the destruction was over, these families had nowhere to go. Employees of the store who were not affected took in displaced residents, and Harry Wolf allowed for a few families to reside at the house on High Street until they could get their lives in order. The store's management team and employees offered assistance by holding a clothing and food drive in the store, as well a collection of money that was then donated to the Red Cross. With the aid of the entire Denholms team, workers could begin the process of rebuilding their lives. Within two years, the city of Worcester had cleaned up and rebuilt the sections that were the hardest hit by the storm. Stricter building codes were enforced to help support both new and existing structures in the event that another storm might hit the area in the future.

By the start of 1954, the city was in better shape, and changes to the look of Main Street were becoming more evident. S.S Kresge, a large discount operation that was located next to Richard Healy in the former Knowles location, purchased the abutting building next to Denholms, which formerly held the women's shop, Slocum's fabrics and a children's store. The dark and ornate five-story brick building was demolished and replaced with a new structure only two levels high to house the Kresge Company. The building consisted of a bleached brick and steel façade with polished stainless accents and large display windows. The north side of Denholms was now exposed, and the brick side wall was

Main Street, Worcester, featuring the S.S. Kresge building and Denholms' new exterior signage.

repointed and then smoothed out to create a large surface, where skilled painters applied a large-scale graphic of the Denholms logo to greet customers as they walked down Main Street. Shoppers were still filling the downtown area at record numbers, and many businesses and offices wanted to capitalize on the more modern approach to exterior design that Denholms had started. More and more façade changes were applied to existing buildings as a way to modernize the structures to fit in with the landscape of the street. By the end of the year, another new look to the avenue would take place.

TREE OF LIGHTS

The previous holiday had been a triumphant one for Denholms, and the buyers and management team were looking to make further financial strides the following Christmas season. Buyers were sent out to New York on buying trips to scout out the most unique offerings to sell to their customers. The holiday season, as any season, was mostly planned out and bought a year in advance, and Harry Wolf wanted to ensure that the store would carry the finest and most exclusive selection of merchandise available in Worcester. With the items being purchased, the next step was to meet with the advertising and display department to focus on a theme for the upcoming window displays and newspaper ads. Harry escorted Eric Hallback across the street, where the pair stood at the end of Franklin Street and gazed at the new façade. "I want the building to look like Christmas," he simply stated. With that direction, it was up to Hallback to come up with a winning design. During previous travels to New York to attend display conferences, Eric had observed what the large department stores there were doing to dress up their buildings for the holidays. The chosen design would be similar to that of Macy's in Herald Square, with a large lit tree on the front elevation of the building.

Hallback and Ted Coghlin of Coghlin Electric finalized the new plans. Coghlin Electric had long been affiliated with Denholms, as the family-owned company had installed all of the interior and exterior electrical work over the years and through its various renovations. The new plan consisted of 2,500 ten-watt bulbs and over two thousand feet of wiring, all of which made up a tree of lights that stood eighty feet high and over seventy feet wide at the base. The tree was topped off with a twelve-foot lit star and grounded on each side with a smaller swag that extended to each side of the building. The windows being planned would tie the new theme together in a uniform package. Smaller exact replicas of the store with the new façade and tree of lights were built and used in each window as the main prop. The children's toy window featured little girls' baby dolls all displayed on shelves of the replica, while the adjoining window featured tartan and velvet dresses and suits for little boys and girls. A women's window tied in with the theme by displaying various nightgowns and peignoir sets all displayed on the shelves of the façade alongside popular perfumes and lotions. All the window sets were installed beneath flocked branches that lined the prosceniums, making for an icy canopy of snow.

When the total design was unveiled, Harry Wolf held an official lighting ceremony outside the store. As dusk approached, massive crowds were formed around the building to gaze at the new spectacle. A single switch illuminated the massive tree, and the glow that it emitted lit up the Main Street block. A choir was assembled outside the building all dressed in green and gold to sing carols to the crowd while they gazed at the tree or stepped closer to marvel at the new window displays. This was the

Left: Denholms' tree of lights. *Courtesy of Henry Dasho.*

Below: A 1954 window display featuring girls' toys.

creation of a new holiday tradition to kick off every Christmas season.

The shoppers' children would also enjoy a newly expanded toy department on the lower level. The large columns that anchored the structure were painted in a red and white candy cane stripe with seven-foot-tall soldiers lining the wide aisles through the department. A ten- by ten-foot table was the main focus, set up with a mechanical train blowing steam and whistles as it made its way through a snowy New England setting. Santa's house was also relocated within the department, and a long corridor alongside the south elevators led parents and children through a winter scene of carriages and flocked trees. When they reached the end of the hallway, a large harlequin-painted wall of red, green and gold framed the scene. Around Santa's velvet throne, oversized candy canes and garlands hung from the ceiling, creating a festive atmosphere for the waiting children. Newly illustrated coloring books showcasing the

A 1954 coloring book.

new façade were handed out to keep the youngsters occupied until it was their turn to sit on Santa's lap.

AFRICAN HOLIDAY

Every year, the promotions at the store were becoming more and more elaborate to draw the customers in. Harry Wolf and the executive team met on a weekly basis with the buyers, department managers and support team to conjure up new ideas. One promotion would revolve around the bridal salon and feature an invitation-only fashion show alongside representatives from the bridal field of expertise. Another event would center on the home furnishings department, where several designers decorated rooms in the Pendleton Shop revolving around traditional, modern and fanciful themes. Speakers would guide customers through the rooms and discuss the latest color schemes that were in fashion and various drapery and carpet treatments, as well as spatial planning. Window display spaces were used to showcase live hairdressing sessions, complete with full makeovers to highlight the seasonal trends in lipstick and shadows, all on view in a live display that was broadcast over speakers installed outside the windows.

One major event a year was planned, and a large budget was assembled to create a storewide event. For 1956, it would take customers on an African Holiday. Denholms would run the promotion storewide through the various departments, as well as advertising and window displays for a four-week period. Above all the cosmetic cases on the ledges were oversized bamboo trellises that framed large images of the map of Africa, with masses of tropical orchids and lilies nestled beneath in planter boxes. The event was carried throughout the upper floors, with displays and signage revolving around the hot colors of oranges and reds accented with magenta and leaf green, all of which highlighted merchandise exclusive to Denholms for the promotion. The entire fleet of delivery trucks received a makeover, with large-scale graphics applied to each side that advertised a thirty-minute color movie that would play on the lower level, featuring actual footage from a real safari adventure. Window displays for the promotion featured a warm orangey red backdrop with large-scale tropical arrangements of flowers and leaves beneath a canopy of large green vines that hung from the ceiling. Mannequins were dressed in silk day dresses in complementary reds and oranges with coordinating hats and accessories. The hand-painted copy for the windows read "Africa's Tiger Lily, A vivid splash of color, a study in fascination and contrast between the spectrums. The beauty of a tiger lily nestled within the cool green depth of the jungle." The overall event was a hit with the customers, and children of all ages made repeat visits to watch the movie that played in a continuous loop.

With space still at a premium in the building, a decision was made to close down the restaurant on the sixth floor. The restaurant had been in use since 1916, when the additional floor was erected alongside the annex expansion. The advertising and display departments were operating out of rented space in an abutting building on Chatham Street that was owned by the YMCA. Relocating these two departments to the upper floor would allow for expansion of each department alongside the beauty salon and would allow for the additional rented space on Chatham Street to be utilized as offices for the buyers and department managers. The restaurant and its tearoom were popular among the customers, and Denholms viewed the closing as a temporary shutdown, with future plans to relocate it to the lower level.

All the interior modifications over the previous decades, including the air conditioning, new sprinkler system and interior lighting, had left pipes exposed that housed the wiring and water necessary for the new systems to operate. Harry Wolf wanted to hide these elements and give each department a cleaner appearance. The decision was made to lower the ceiling height throughout the store by a foot and a half and lower the large fluorescent fixtures that illuminated the building to create a flush surface. A large team of workmen, as well as the Coghlin Electric Company, worked in stages throughout the store. Large scaffolding was erected so workers could lay the new support structure that would hold up the ceiling. Alongside the team, each of the four-by-four lighting fixtures would be dropped and reaffixed to the new network of supports and cables, making for a long and tedious process. Daily meetings with the executive team and the project manager would determine which department would be done next so as not to interfere with current promotions or events being held in the store. Within a year, the entire store was retrofitted with the new ceiling, which only added to the store's modern approach to design.

Chapter 10
The Early '60s

In 1960, the company suffered another internal loss. Paul Wolf passed away due to long-term complications from cancer. After only eight years with the Denholm and McKay Company, Paul Wolf was remembered for being a hard worker, extremely focused on the operational side of the business and a kind man. The loss was felt throughout the entire store and by Harry on a more personal level.

By 1961, things were looking brighter for the Denholm and McKay Company. To celebrate another outstanding year for the store, Harry Wolf held a large gala reception for the executives, buyers and management of the store. The event was held on April 30 at the Bancroft Hotel, which was located on Franklin Street in the downtown area. Situated in the grand ballroom, the attendees were treated to a lavish meal, as well as flowing cocktails, all revolving around various speeches and milestones, such as the achievement of departments that met or exceeded plan. Recipients were handed small corsages of orchids and tuberose all held neatly in small gold vials, which were pinned to sharply tailored suits or the cocktail dresses they wore. The event was also to pay tribute to Elsie McCarthy, who was retiring later that season after an extensive employment with the company. McCarthy had started her career with Denholms in 1921 and had worked her way up the ranks with responsibilities in the buying office over women's sportswear, dresses, evening and bridal. Harry Wolf gave a heartfelt speech about the role that she had played with the company and her many successes. As a farewell gift, the management team showered her with a lavish spray of roses alongside a crystal bowl engraved with her years of service.

Denholms' principle areas of focus were the women's departments, as they offered the greatest volume of sales and always maintained a healthy margin for the store. The proper candidate would need to be found to ensure continued success. It wasn't until summer that a replacement was named. Her name was Josephine Carbone, or simply Jo, as her peers would call her. Carbone had joined the store in the fall of 1947 and started her career as a stock girl. With a passion for retail and a love of fashion, she quickly made her way up the corporate ladder. Promotions throughout the years from department manager to assistant buyer and then buyer of women's sportswear gave her the necessary background to fill the position. In her new role, she would be responsible for all aspects of buying and managing within the evening and daytime dresses, the bridal salon and the Salisbury Shop (Denholms' higher-priced salon),

Harry Wolf and Elsie McCarthy during her retirement party.

along with women's sportswear, juniors and blouses. She was also put in charge of coordinating the various fashion shows and interviews with the local media.

Denholms was a full-service store and wanted to keep shoppers in the building for as long as it could. With the need for lunch or dinner, patrons and employees would often leave the store and go across the street to Toupins restaurant or travel to Putnam and Thurston's to grab a bite to eat. After the closing in 1957, plans to reopen the restaurant were analyzed, and the proper space needed to be allocated. In December 1961, the restaurant and tearoom reopened but was now relocated to the lower level. The new space would occupy 2,600 square feet and serve full hot meals, as well as lighter fare, in a modern setting of bleached maple wood with accents of aqua and tangerine art dotting the perimeter walls. The new space was leased out to the John F. Davis Company, which ran thirteen other restaurants and tearooms with the various Allied, May Company and Interstate department stores across the country. The dining area was an immediate success, and it allowed the store to hold informal modeling while guests dined and enjoyed a break from a day of shopping.[15] Ted Kennedy, a young senator at the time, would often frequent the new restaurant during trips out to Worcester and would arrange to have lunch with Russell Corsini where the two would talk about politics and business affairs over an unpretentious lunch of sandwiches and coffee.

By 1963, the social climate in the city was starting to change. Large groups of activists were protesting across the country and also in the city of Worcester to proclaim equal rights toward blacks. D'Army Bailey headed up the organization of protesters and contacted the management team at Denholms to question their lack of blacks in upper management roles. Denholms had a strict nondiscriminatory policy of hiring, which the group did not feel was being upheld. Mary Loughlin was the director of personnel for the store, and most of the communication had been filtered through her. At the time, Denholms employed 533 associates. Out of the 533 people employed, only 16 were African American. They consisted of 8 elevator operators, 4 matrons, 2 beauty salon maids, 1 stock clerk and 1 shoe repairman. In the store's ninety-one-year history, only 1 black person had been promoted above the blue-collar level. When the talks between the two sides failed to reach common ground, a protest was organized against the Denholm and McKay Company. A large group of picketers formed outside the Denholms store with large signs in hand. In an effort to try to negotiate some peace, Harry Wolf went outside with refreshments and asked for the group to come in and have a discussion. When the conversation ended, Denholms agreed to reevaluate its hiring practices. Wolf also approached each of the store's African American employees and asked them if there were any other positions that they would like to obtain. Each of them stated that they were fairly compensated for their jobs and did not want to make any moves within the organization. Going forward, Denholms would hire and promote regardless of race, sex or age. The company also began to post any job openings within the store so employees would have a fair shot before they were offered to outside candidates.

High Street

Later that same year, a more ambitious expansion was underway. The former High Street receiving dock that was in the rear of the building was now being relocated to the Chase Court, which ran underneath the store through an alley behind the Richard Healy store. The new expansion would add an additional twenty-five thousand square feet of selling space and allow for an expansion of the children's department, as well as a newly formed junior high shop. The new entrance would be designed by the architectural firm of H.E. Davidson & Sons, which had done the front façade in the early 1950s, and constructed by the Bozenhard Company out of Shrewsbury, Massachusetts. The plans called for a two-story limestone façade with an eighty-foot marquee capping off two newly formed display windows. A large, stainless steel, back-lighted sign in the Denholms script would mark the new entrance. In order to give the building the necessary space it needed to make the expansion possible, the former brick house purchased in 1952 was demolished and converted into parking spaces for the store's use.

The Story of Worcester's Premier Department Store

Alongside the High Street entrance expansion, Denholms also purchased the former YWCA building, which was located on Chatham Street abutting the store. The former gymnasium consisted of two structures. The first structure was erected in 1891 and had been designed by the architectural firm of Earle and Fuller, which also designed the original façade for the Denholm and McKay Company in 1881. Alongside that building was a 1915 brick and glass edifice designed by George Clemence. Work began on the former YWCA spaces to even out the floors so they matched the elevation of the existing store, and small mezzanines were added to offset any change in floor height between the two buildings. The former pool on the second floor was boarded over and kept intact to allow for possible reuse at some point. The addition of space would allow for expansion of the women's sportswear department to create the Country Shop, which featured blouses and sweaters all showcased in a setting reminiscent of a quaint New England house with shingled walls and large, antique, black lanterns illuminating the department. A full epicure department would also be added, which would feature gourmet treats and wines, alongside an expanded candy department featuring the Russell Stover line of candy, which was sold exclusively at the time by Denholms. The fabric and notions department would also have new housing on the first floor of the Chatham building in a modern, sleek setting of teak wood and chrome fixtures that housed the endless array of fabrics being offered.

The younger generations were becoming more important to sales of the store in the early 1960s. Previously, the smaller sizes had been housed in the women's departments and cut in the same fabric as offered to the older clientele. The new generation wanted youthful fabrics and smaller sizes to emulate what was being shown abroad on the British runways. With the growing expansion of this age group, a newly formed Junior High Loft catered to the younger consumers in the former YWCA space on the third floor. The up-to-the-minute department featured a record player, a Coke machine and a recently fashioned advisory board where members could talk about new and upcoming trends in clothing and music, as well as school life. The setting of this department featured a relaxed outdoor environment complete with park benches and large mannequin displays posed around oversized maple trees and local school pennants.

With the acquirement of the new building came the possibility for additional parking. The original 1891 structure abutting the newly renovated space was raised to allow for a forty-unit parking lot to be built on the former foundation. Space in the city was at a premium, and more shoppers were adopting automobiles as their choice of transportation. With the lack of parking, Denholms was afraid that it would lose shoppers to the suburban malls that were popping up in surrounding towns. With the building leveled, the exposed exterior walls were then repointed and painted a bright white with large Denholms logos applied on each focal wall to create a unified appearance. The new parking lot alongside the High Street entrance offered customers greater ease to access the store, and the term "one-store shopping" was applied to newspaper and radio advertisements to announce the newly formed space.

The former High Street receiving dock. Pictured to the left is the brick house purchased by the Denholm and McKay Company.

The new High Street entrance dressed up for the holidays. *From the collections of the Worcester Historical Museum, Worcester, Massachusetts.*

The new fabric and notions department located on Chatham 1. *Courtesy of the* Worcester Telegram and Gazette.

Parking beside Denholms' High Street entrance. *Courtesy of the* Worcester Telegram and Gazette.

The front façade also received a new look with two bronze flagpoles anchored into the limestone slabs. As a way to commemorate the store's Scottish roots, Wolf enlisted Hallback to design a new flag that would be the store's motto. The design featured a royal purple background with a gold belt forming a circular frame around an illustration of Scottish thistle (which had been used in the store's early days in advertisements and postcards). Around the frame were the Latin words "Nemo Me Impune Lacessit," which translates to "No one attacks me with impunity." The flag waved proudly alongside the United States flag and was only removed due to bad weather conditions or the lighting of the Christmas tree on the building.

Escal-Aires

Originally, Denholms' seven floors were operated by five service elevators located on the perimeter walls of the building. With the expansion of High Street, the traffic pattern in the store was being weighted to the elevator walls and not down center aisles, which contained some of the store's higher-profile departments, such as cosmetics. Harry Wolf consulted with Alice Silagri, a stockholder in Denholms and an associate with the Otis Elevator Company. The Otis Company met with Wolf to discuss plans to reroute traffic through the center of the building and allow for greater and faster ease to the upper floors. The design would include two separate banks of escalators so as not to add more strain on the 1881 building. In order to keep the design light and airy, a new product called the "Escal-Aire" would be installed. The new glass escalators would feature a stainless steel and aluminum base structure with charcoal handrails. The most impressive feature would be the exclusive rococo-style decoration hand applied on each pane of glass sandwiched between two other panes to prevent scratching to the design. The cost was exorbitant, but Wolf wanted to be able to service the customers in an elegant format. These were the first Escal-Aires to be installed in the New England area, and Denholms was the first store in Worcester to have an escalator in its building, so every detail needed to be correct. With an older structure, surveys were done to map out where the banks of escalators would sit. It was determined that floors one through three would have the new glass Escal-Aires centered within the store. Floors three through five would adopt a more traditional steel and aluminum housing painted a soft blue, which would be located in the center of the third floor to distribute the weight more evenly. With all plans approved, workmen started the yearlong task of reinforcing the floors, cutting massive holes and assembling the new mode of transportation through the store. With the escalators being constructed, new floor plans were executed to update the women's third floor, as well as key areas around the store where the escalators would pick up and drop off customers.

The new design featured reorganized interiors throughout the store. The dress department was remodeled in a light green color palette, with large applied wall moldings above the soffits and on the three cocoa brown display walls that highlighted the perfectly coiffed mannequins. For the ladies' evening wear shop, a more formal presence was made by the seven-foot crystal chandelier that was suspended above a large floral arrangement of white lilies, roses and freesia. A new and updated

Salisbury Shop received a teak wood and gold leaf ironwork entrance, and the interior was fitted with a small settee upholstered in soft taupe leather and a gold ornate side table adorned with the latest fashion magazines. A large platform was erected between two of the newly mirrored support columns and used for fashion shows as well as mannequin presentations. Gold leaf case lines were added to the floor to highlight small rhinestone clutches, gloves and jewelry that coordinated with the various evening gowns and cocktail dresses.

By the north bank of elevators, a separate Capezio shoe salon was added, and a formal Blouse Bar was installed where customers would find the finest silk blouses neatly folded within the new chrome and glass case lines. In the women's sportswear department, a new swing shop was installed where merchandise would change out seasonally to reflect current trends. The shop was renovated with large bleached pine raised panel walls, oversized palladium mirrors and a large traditional glass hurricane chandelier. In December, one could find an assortment of pastel cruise wear residing in the area, and by late spring, it would convert to a swim shop, complete with straw hats and tote bags. Fall would usually bring wool kilts and coordinating sweater sets, all displayed among large autumnal arrangements of leaves and branches.

The fur salon was also expanded and encased in a large black framework of decorative iron scrollwork and set against scarlet upholstered walls with black Louis armchairs with gold leaf details. Also on the third floor was the newly installed young men's Varsity Shop, where collegiate suits and top coats were merchandised with skinny rep ties and cardigan sweaters, all housed in an ivy row setting. The fourth-floor gift and china departments were expanded and painted a soft, airy blue with new glossy white floor fixtures and small glass vitrines showcasing higher price point giftables. Large formal dining tables appointed with fine china, along with the appropriate stemware and flatware, gave shoppers creative tablescaping ideas to transform their own dining rooms. On the fifth floor, a newly expanded and renovated television and radio department showcased the massive collection of electronics that was offered at the store, along with the new oak and glass listening booths that were erected to allow shoppers to sample the vast array of records in a soundproof environment.

Right: The first-floor up Escal-Aire, 1964.

Below: Denholms' Swing Shop, located on the third floor behind women's sportswear.

With the construction of the escalators advancing through the fall and holiday season, floors one through three were opened up with the new transportation in March 1964 (floors three through five would open later that year). The store held a large press conference and ribbon-cutting ceremony heralding the triumph with the newspapers and via radio interviews. The Otis Elevator Company, which manufactured all the new escalators, was on hand to photograph the executive team alongside the Escal-Aires and include the store in its marketing campaigns. The design was a hit from day one. Shoppers were thrilled at the ease and grace that they added to the building, and for many, it was their first time riding an escalator. Denholms took out a six-page spread in the *Worcester Telegram* announcing the new mode of transportation, as well as the other interior improvements around the store. The *Worcester Telegram* itself ran photos showcasing shoppers arriving on the down Escal-Aire to the first floor with the store's newly designed shopping bags in hand. The bag

A graphic of a
Denholms shopping bag.

Eric Hallback greeting
customers on the new
Escal-Aires.

consisted of a simple hand drawing of the façade of the building done in
aqua set against a white, lustrous backdrop. The store's management and
associates were thrilled and proud of what the store had accomplished.
The escalators were a major investment and marked another form of
advancement in the retailer's ninety-three-year history.

Chapter 11
Changing Times

By the summer of 1966, the store was operating on strong financial ground. With the need to continually expand and promote the business, Harry Wolf promoted Eric Hallback to display director over promotions and windows. In addition to the promotion of Hallback, three new stylists were added to the display team to help execute the growing number of promotions and window displays that changed out every two weeks. To help facilitate these changes, Denholms hired Robert Branczyk to be in charge of the window and interior displays, reporting to Hallback. Branczyk was an established stylist, having worked as a freelancer for the Korey's store, as well as display assistant at the Hecht Company based in Washington, D.C. His keen eye for details and styling made him the perfect candidate to maintain the upscale image of the store. Alongside Branczyk was another new hire by the name of Bernice Salmonsen, a graduate of the Worcester Art Museum who was friendly with Hallback. In her new role, she would be the fashion coordinator over the windows and interior mannequin displays. The third stylist was Irving Bostock. Bostock had his initial training working for a window treatment store for ten years, where he executed the various displays. He would now be responsible for all the interior displays and trim under Branczyk. Wolf and Russell Corsini understood the importance that the displays contributed to the store's overall image and business and that the window displays often sold more than newspaper advertisements.

Denholms' display department. *Left to right*: Eric Hallback, Bernice Salmonsen, Bob Branczyk and Irving Bostock.

The first promotion under Hallback's direction was called "The World at Your Door." The event centered on the assorted imported merchandise that the buyers had assembled over the past year from around the globe. The goods consisted of fine Italian cashmere sweaters and throws, Belgian-made glass and ceramics, French provincial furniture sets and exotic skin handbags, to name a few. The storewide event tied in with the British Overseas Airway Corporation, and the store erected a kiosk on the fourth floor where customers could meet with a travel representative and book a future trip or enter a raffle for a winning prize of a week's stay at the Carlton Beach resort in Bermuda. On the fourth floor outside the fine china department, a large bronze water fountain was installed in a tropical garden-like setting where shoppers could throw their extra change and make a wish to support UNICEF. Throughout the store, oversized pennant banners of the respective countries were used to decorate the main floor and participating departments. Swagged from column to column, they created archways leading the customers down

Denholms' third-floor millinery department, circa 1966.

the main aisles throughout the store. On top of the store's cosmetic and handbag ledges, mile markers of how far each European city was from Worcester were displayed alongside a mannequin dressed in the finest imported fashion and ready for travel abroad. On top of the exterior marquee, a row of flagpoles with the corresponding countries billowed in the wind and reinforced the storewide promotion. The event was a winning triumph, and customers flocked to the store to purchase the assorted goods being offered for a limited time.

With the fall selling season off to a financial success, another emotional blow affected the store significantly. On September 22, 1966, during a round of golf, Harry Wolf passed away unexpectedly from a heart attack. Not since the loss of Frank Krim had the store mourned so deeply. At fifty-nine years of age, Wolf would be remembered for his contributions to the expansion and modernization of the building, as well as for his love of the store and the employees who worked for him. During the mourning period, the display team paid respect by installing a window display in commemoration of Wolf, complete with a large portrait of him together with a Bible and oversized candles. A small sign at the base of the display offered the store's condolences to the family of their fallen leader. As another form of remembrance, the store's employees gathered a collection of money and commissioned Emil Grilli to produce a bronze plaque to be erected in remembrance of Wolf's commitment and dedication to the store. Grilli, who was a talented artist, sculpture and painter, had long been associated with the Denholm and McKay Company as the main artist who hand painted all the store's signage and window copy. The final design was a bronze plaque measuring twenty-eight inches wide by thirty-six inches tall with a sculpted likeness of Harry Wolf, and underneath it read "HARRY F. WOLF President of Denholm and McKay, 1946–1966, Placed here in loving memory by the Denholm employees." The plaque was soon erected on the main floor staircase by the handbag and glove department.

With Harry Wolf's passing, the board of directors named Russell Corsini to be his replacement as general manager of the Denholm and McKay Company, and board member Alexander Keys was named president. Corsini had been with the store since 1938 and fully understood the inner workings of the company and how to propel it into the future years. With his personal and professional attachment to the company, shareholders and the Scottish Trading Company felt comfortable with the transition of power. With Corsini moving up in the ranks, this allowed for two other associates to have career advancements with the company. The first was John McLoughlin Jr., who had started his career with Denholms in 1956 as the department manager of housewares. Before Denholms, McLoughlin was a graduate of St. Peters and had worked for the John MacInnes Company for ten years. In his new role, he would become merchandise manager

Russell Corsini. *Courtesy of the Corsini family.*

of all the hard lines in the store. These areas included small electrics, appliances, furniture, housewares, fine china and giftables, cosmetics and fragrances, epicure and rugs. The other promotion as merchandise manager over all soft goods was given to Josephine Carbone. Carbone would be responsible for all women's and men's sportswear, dresses, suiting, bridal, men's furnishings and suiting, shoes, intimate apparel, children's, millinery, coats and furs. With a new management team in place, the first order of business was the anniversary of the "World at Your Door" event and planning of the next all-store promotion.

Expo '67

In April 1967, the store was transformed into a tribute to the World's Fair named "Expo '67, the Universal and International Exhibit of Canada." The store's Main Street window run showcased a traveling retrospective of what visitors to the Expo '67 exhibit would find amid an array of merchandise tailored toward the customer who travels. As part of the promotion for the event, Parisian fashions were flown in and showcased in the store's fashion windows. Amid a backdrop of red, white and blue felt streamers and gold leaf fleur de lis, mannequins were dressed in the latest styles. Each of the ensembles was designed by new and upcoming designers that Denholms would carry in the higher-end Salisbury Shop. The outfits consisted of tailored feminine suits with glove-length sleeves and tight pencil skirts, all shown with coordinating hats and handbags.

When customers entered into the store, large-scale graphics of the World's Fair designed by Montreal artist Julien Hebert showed simple vertical line drawings with outstretched arms set in pairs to represent friendship around the world. These graphics were used storewide to draw attention to special displays highlighting man's contributions and developments to the world. The first floor consisted of a special fine arts exhibit focusing on man's achievements in photography, contemporary sculpture and industrial design. On the third floor by the up escalators, glass vitrines were placed down the main aisle and the exhibits centered on the subject "Man the Explorer." Each display case focused on a different subject, i.e., man and his planet and space, man and the polar regions

A fifth-floor exhibit during the Expo '67 event.

A Main Street window display featuring women's fashions during the Expo '67 event.

and man and the oceans. The event carried through the store to the fifth floor, where a section of the store was converted into a large walk-through exhibit of the event. As an anchor to the theme, customers could view a large-scale, three-dimensional model of the city of Montreal, complete with the various pavilions and architecture erected for the event. As another travel tie-in, the store raffled off a free five-day holiday for two, complete with all the trimmings, to view the actual exhibit. During the event, organizers of the world fair and representatives from the Canadian government came to view the exhibit at Denholms and commended Russell Corsini and Eric Hallback for the design and execution of the storewide retrospective.

Following on the heels of the Expo '67 event was a visit to the store from Mrs. Demitri Pondosoupolis, the Greek consul's wife. In preparation for the event, Denholms did a special buy of merchandise made and exported from Greece. Brightly colored pottery and embossed metal decoratives bought by Lillian MacNeil were showcased in the china and gift departments alongside representatives who gave in-depth lectures about how each piece was produced and the special characteristics they possessed. On the lower level, an authentic Greek bakery was set up and run by the Saint Spyridon Church and served traditional Greek specialties such as baklava, kataifi and powdered kourabiedes. In the store's main windows, mannequins were outfitted in the latest fashions inspired by Greek design. These outfits were juxtaposed alongside traditionally dressed mannequins wearing authentic costumes such as Crete's and Foustanella's/Tsolias. Throughout the store, large abstract Grecian columns decorated the main floor and were used to highlight the displays of merchandise that had been imported for the event. On the third floor by the north bank of elevators, an official Greek dance troupe performed traditional dances in bright red and gold Karagounas to a crowd of customers. Throughout the week during the limited event, fashion shows and art lectures were held to highlight the country of Greece and educate the consumer on its culture.

The store did not solely rely on promotions to drive business. The important interactions between the customers and the associates were Denholms' main focus. Special training classes were held for new and existing sales associates to help them develop the best customer service

A luncheon in honor of the Greek consul's wife. *Left to right*: Eric Hallback, Bessie Lagadinos, Ann Scarlata (secretary to consul's wife), Reverend Tsanikos, Mrs. Demitri Pendosoupolis (consul's wife), Josephine Carbone, Russell Corsini and Charles Davis.

standards available. As a form of good business practice, associates would hand write thank-you notes to customers after their purchases were complete. Follow-up phone calls were also made to alert clients to upcoming sales, new product deliveries or just to wish them a happy birthday. The relationship of the store with the community is what made Denholms' service standards of the highest regard. The buying team, along with store management, listened to associates during morning meetings and round table discussions to see what the buying public was asking for. As a form of reward, customer letters praising the service received were posted by the lower-level time clock for all to read. Oftentimes during his daily walk-throughs of the store, Russell Corsini would congratulate associates on a letter received or coach them on how to give better service the next time they interacted with a customer.

Another form of good service was made by the store's generous return policy. If a purchase was made that the customer did not feel

A window display for the Greek fashion odyssey promotion.

represented the best quality or proper fit, the store would take it back without hesitation. The store even accepted the return of an entire box of chocolates that was fully eaten when the customer stated that she just wasn't fond of the candy. Denholms prided itself on the service standards that it implemented and constantly strived to exceed customer expectations. When a bridal party of dresses was delayed from the manufacturer in New York, bridal manager Therease O'Laughlin waited at the local Greyhound station until the dresses arrived via bus at 10:00 p.m. Once the dresses were retrieved, she then drove them to the anxious bridal party and assisted with any last-minute alterations so the wedding could take place the following day.

The customer service that the store provided also extended outside of the store's environment. Russell Corsini played an active role in the Worcester Chamber of Commerce, donating his time and knowledge to help assist other retailers and companies prosper in the city. Denholms also made large monetary contributions to the city's various charities and civic projects to better enhance the downtown area. As the largest retailer in the heart of the city, the store felt it was its responsibility to actively participate in the growth and prosperity of the city it called home.

During the same time period, the city of Worcester was starting to change. In 1967, the population of Worcester had dropped slightly to 176,572, and residents were leaving the city for larger dwellings and single-family homes in the neighboring towns. The rise of suburbia was a nationwide issue for retailers, as large downtown flagship stores were starting to feel the competition from suburban shopping malls that were opening up around the country at a growing pace. To help revitalize the downtown core, a new $45 million business and commercial complex was being planned and named the Worcester Center Galleria. The new mall would concentrate shoppers from Main Street to the new center, which would be situated on Front Street near the commons. The plans would include 2 main anchor stores, 175 smaller boutique stores, restaurants, a theater and parking for four thousand cars. The organizers of the mall approached Russell Corsini about relocating Denholms into the new complex. Presently, Filene's was the only tenant signed on to be an anchor store, and the mall needed to lock in another main store to secure funding. During the discussion stages, the mall developers informed Corsini that they planned on relocating as many stores from the Main Street area to the new mall as possible and that the existing leased spaces of those stores would be left unoccupied. Corsini was apprehensive about the new mall and didn't feel that it would have longevity within the city. He also felt that Denholms was established in its proper location and didn't want to abandon the company's history by vacating the Main Street premises that had been erected for it. With a formal rejection by Denholms to join the complex, the mall proceeded to fill the space with the Jordan Marsh Company, which was based in Boston and had several branch stores throughout New England.

Chapter 12
Retail as Theater

By the start of 1968, the fashion industry was changing dramatically. The introduction of the mini skirt was at the time a fashion revolution. New silhouettes, including the maxi skirt and maxi dress, also came into play as a contradiction to the sometimes seventeen-inch skirt lengths. With the fashion direction coming from Britain and the teen population growing at an alarming rate, the world was a changing place. New models such as Twiggy, with her flat, almost boyish figure, replaced the fuller-figured icons in the industry. As part of the youth craze, Denholms began an expansion of its departments serving the younger clientele. "They're thinking style when they're in grammar school," Russell Corsini remarked in a newspaper interview. After several buying trips to New York in which Corsini and Josephine Carbone analyzed the current trends in place at Bloomingdale's and other high-end stores, the decision was made to reorient its presentation of merchandise in the women's and juniors departments and create smaller boutique shops. Each of these shops would be completely renovated and offer a personalized assortment of merchandise geared to a specific clientele. The shops would all be given a name to further enhance the boutique environment. For the younger generation, a new Place on 3 Mod Shop would offer the latest in cutting-edge fashions, from mini skirts to patent leather go-go boots to brightly colored panty hose. In stark contrast to the modern apparel was the Poise-N-Ivy shop, which catered to the refined collegiate shopper and carried wool blazers, pleated kilt skirts, knee-high socks and penny loafers. In the women's dress department, a new Import Boutique featured gifts, jewelry, perfumes and custom apparel.

To further enhance the interior of the store, Corsini began a large-scale renovation in partnership with the head of store planning, Atilio Alinovi, to update the entire main floor of the store, beginning with a new men's suits and furnishings department. The new design would feature pine-paneled walls, leather club chairs, new wood and glass bunkers to house suits and an oversized oil painting of a hunt scene to complete the gentlemen's atmosphere. In addition to the men's renovations, all the columns on the first floor were boxed in to create a unified appearance. Over the years, new columns were added to support the sixth floor and the introduction of the escalators. These newer columns did not have the original scalloped details that the 1882 columns possessed. The updated column design would feature a simple faux strie design in off-white, with a simple gold molding trim. To coordinate with the new columns, the

The women's third-floor gift boutique, located in the women's dress department by the down escalator.

The renovated first floor, showcasing the new custom-made Karastan worsted wool (Kirman) Persian rug. *From the collections of the Worcester Historical Museum, Worcester, Massachusetts.*

perimeter walls were repainted in a soft taupe color scheme, with gold and off-white accent walls. The most impressive change was in the flooring. The rectangular tiles from 1951 were getting worn out, and Corsini wanted to add a greater sense of elegance to the first floor. The chosen design to resurface the entire first floor was a custom-made Karastan worsted wool (Kirman) Persian rug in multicolored jewel tones. The end product would transform the entire floor into a luxurious shopping environment fitted in the highest of quality.

The interior and window displays were also getting more elaborate in their approach. One season, shoppers might find oversized gold birdcages on all the first-floor ledges with animatronic birds chirping. Another design would feature gilded cherubs holding up large crystal sconces affixed to each of the columns. Other displays would tie into specific cosmetic events where striped gazebos adorned with fringe trimmings sat next to life-size Greek statues to announce the launch of a new, intimate line of perfumes. The window displays during this time were getting more thematic as well. Complete stories were being told with propping and merchandise. A window display for London Fog raincoats would show a mannequin leaning up against an antique street lamp with a skyline of London illuminated in the background. At her feet would be a large convincing puddle with a sign card stating, "The completely versatile all weather travel coat." Another fashion window might feature a new fleet of mannequins purchased to highlight the new mod high-fashion trends. With their slim faces, elongated torsos and '60s makeup, they were often posed against modern furniture settings consisting of Mylar papered walls and Lucite furniture. After a major accident during the Christmas season in 1967, when two automobiles crashed through the main windows at the end of Franklin Street, a new, high-end lighting system was installed throughout all the store windows during the renovations. The new tracks were of theater grade and had the ability to alter the lighting by use of colored gels and projected images. The new lighting system would help the display team convey a mood or highlight specific details on the merchandise.

Most of the display budgets were allocated for main promotions throughout the year, while the bulk of the dollars were spent on the costly holiday windows and interior displays. The process of converting the store into Christmas mode took months of preparation to coordinate themes and procure new propping. Starting in early November, the display department, with the assistance of interns, would begin hanging the holiday trim on the fifth floor. When that level was completed, the next floor down would be transformed into holiday mode. At the end of the process, there would be a grand unveiling of the main-floor holiday trim, which opened for the public to view on black Friday. The first-floor design changed yearly. One theme was an ice-encased design where large, realistic icicles were hung, forming massive archways down the main aisles. The columns were then wrapped in a silver reflective material, on which concealed lighting projected falling water. Another year, it was more conventional in design, when the main columns were padded out in rich red velvet with plaster cherubs holding up small trees affixed to each side. Large garland swags of greenery filled with crystals and pearls were anchored to traditional cut crystal chandeliers with red pleated shades. The first floor during the main holidays was always the most impressive in its design, and a large portion of the budget used for the interiors was allocated to trimming out the street level.

Along with the interiors, the Main Street windows were also the most extravagant during the holiday season. Displays featuring specially designed animated snowmen and young children formed fantasy windows set in a frosty candy land scene. With no merchandise placed in these windows, they were designed for the children of the city to view and be enthralled by the moving objects and glittery props. Alongside the animatronic windows were displays allocated to adult gift giving. Large archways of lit and heavily decorated pine garlands framed out vignettes showcasing women's evening gowns, men's formal wear and assorted accessories shown in a formal residential setting. These window displays often revolved around specific themes or colors and would completely

The Christmas window displays along the Main Street entrance to Denholms.

The main floor of Denholms decked out for the Christmas season. *Courtesy of Bob Branczyk and Irving Bostock.*

change concepts from year to year. The large lit tree that adorned the building would also receive periodic changes. One season, all red bulbs would be used. Another year might feature green bulbs forming the tree and clear bulbs as the garland swags on either side. Since its incarnation in 1955, the tree of lights had helped Denholms draw crowds of shoppers into the store to view the festive window displays. It had also become an icon for the city of Worcester.

As a form of educating the consumer on the changing trends in fashion, Denholms started to hold more fashion shows than it had in previous years. The shows were coordinated by Josephine Carbone and were held in store as well as around the city, where they would tie in with various charity groups. The in-store shows were featured on the third floor in the dress and evening departments and would often highlight the new trends of the season or a particular department, such as bridal or evening wear. Large crowds of shoppers would file in and be seated in the rows of folding chairs set up alongside the runway. Here, shoppers could get their first view of the latest fashions that were being shown in the magazines of the day and how Denholms was interpreting the trends. Models would walk casually onto the runway dressed from head to toe and completely accessorized with hats, gloves and purses. The commentary for these shows was done by Carbone, who was usually perched at a podium erected for the shows. As each model filed out, a complete description of the outfit and accessories was dictated to the large crowd that had assembled. Oftentimes, the local media and photographers were on hand to snap pictures of each model to showcase in the various articles written for the newspapers.

To coincide with the in-store shows, a formal Fashion Advisory Board was set up and run by the Capezio Shoe Company to attract younger generations of students to get involved with the store and shop the

Model Linda Gravlin.

new juniors department. To qualify for the fashion board, each student needed to fill out a questionnaire and complete an essay on school life and social activities. The students were then handpicked by the board members, including representatives from Capezio Shoes and *Seventeen* magazine and Eric Hallback. The students foremost responsibilities were to educate the younger clientele on new fashion trends within the store, participate in formal fashion shows and garner other students to shop at Denholms. The chosen students were also groomed to take on additional management responsibilities upon graduation from college. One such participant was Linda Gravlin, who started her career with Denholms in 1965 working part time in the stockrooms. As an active member of the Fashion Advisory Board, she was one of the store's premier models and was featured at all Denholms in-store and remote fashion shows. Gravlin

Josephine Carbone commentating during a Denholms fashion show.

continued with Denholms after graduation, when she further advanced her career working as a buyer alongside Carbone. Her continued success with the store stemmed from the education that she received in school, as well as her training on the Fashion Advisory Board.

THE ITALIAN EVENT

For the fall of 1968, the store partnered with the Italian Trade Commission to produce an event that would expose customers to merchandise made and exported from Italy. The Italian Trade Commission studied Denholms for two years before giving the green light to the event. The commission looked at the store's merchandise assortment and vendor matrix, as well as the budget that would be allocated to host the event. In order to have the proper merchandise in place, Russell Corsini, along with Josephine Carbone, traveled to Italy to meet with the vendors and analyze the assortments. Traveling alongside Corsini was his wife, Elizabeth, as well as his sister-in-law Ann. The trade commission offered suggestions for products that it felt would be well tailored to the Worcester clientele. Cashmere sweaters made of the finest Italian wool, brightly colored Majolica pottery and handmade men's Italian suits were a fraction of the buy. In order to create a buzz in the city and get additional press, Carbone bought an exclusive Italian line of dresses and separates that would be sold in the Salisbury Shop on the third floor. The most notable item was a hand-embroidered evening pantsuit made out of black wool crepe, heavily encrusted with jewels and beading. The suit retailed for $3,500 (at 1968 prices) and garnered an article in the local newspapers announcing the arrival of the couture fashions to the Worcester store. The windows for the event featured mannequins dressed in wool knit dresses with fur and mohair accessories. The men's windows featured fine Italian tailored suits and sport coats with the new broader lapels. Coordinating dress shirts and woven ties completed the men's ensembles, and fine leather shoes and small accessories were displayed to finish off the look.

To create an environment for the merchandise, large, three-dimensional graphics of Italian architecture were assembled to give a dramatic effect to the window displays. To kick off the event, the store held wine tastings, which featured selections from Italian vineyards during a private reception. As a backdrop for the event, musicians were stationed by the main escalators playing classical music, while informal models walked throughout the store dressed in Italian sportswear and couture. To create the appropriate environment within the store, Italian flags were hung from the main-floor columns, along with red, white and green felt streamers that were artfully swaged from the ceiling. On top of the main ledges behind the various case lines, arrangements of olive branches, laurel leaves and dried filler formed topiaries inspired by the gardens of Italy. In the gourmet shop on Chatham Street, Italian pastries, olive oils and wines were added to the assortment for customers to sample as well as purchase

Left to right: Ann Corsini, Josephine Carbone, Elizabeth (Krim) Corsini and Russell Corsini on a buying trip for the storewide Italian event.

The Denholms window display for the Denholms Italian event. *Courtesy of Bob Branczyk and Irving Bostock.*

during the event. From the lower level—where representatives from the various cookware lines served Italian foods during demonstrations—to the bedding department—where Italian linens were artfully displayed—all areas of the store were involved to generate an authentic environment.

Chapter 13
One Hundred Years Young

The management at Denholms had always contemplated opening a branch store in the past but couldn't secure the proper location. During the midsummer months of 1968, Russell Corsini was approached by the First Hartford Realty Corporation based in Manchester, Connecticut. The group was planning to build a $9 million shopping mall in Auburn, Massachusetts, near Drury Square. The realty company had been in negotiations with Sears Roebuck and wanted Denholms to be the upscale anchor in the mall. After months of demographic studies, a determination was made that Auburn would be a suitable fit without drawing on the Worcester customer base. Denholms signed on to be an anchor alongside Sears, and a projected opening of spring 1970 was announced to the public.[16] Work was slated to break ground in December of that year and would coincide with the completion of the I-290 interstate, which would connect Worcester to Auburn in a fifteen-minute drive.

Coinciding with the planning stages was a reorganization within the company. The families of Frank Krim and Harry and Paul Wolf, as well as a private investor, had been in negotiations to sell their controlling interest to a conglomerate with ties to Waltham and Providence. The sale of Denholms included the assets (including the name), as well as the real estate that housed the store; the private corporate stock was not included. A new, separate holding company appropriately named Denkay was formed for the investment of the stores and would be headed by Russell Corsini. The new controlling corporation, named Mayflower Properties, was run by Howard N. Feist, who was a native of Weston, Massachusetts, and owner of Gladdings department store in Providence, Rhode Island; New England Mica Company of Waltham; Avery Piano Corporation of Providence; and Dover's Incorporated out of Westerly, Rhode Island. Under the acquisition, Denholms would now be part of a larger group of stores and thus would allow for greater buying power. As part of the acquisition, Corsini, who previously had been executive vice-president and general manager, would now become president of Denholms, succeeding Alexander Keyes. A new Denholms executive committee was named, including Corsini; Feist as chairman of Denholms and Gladdings; and Leonard Johnson, who would now be a chairman of Denholms as well as president of Gladdings. As part of the merger, Denholms would retain its own identity and maintain its internal management structure to allow the store to operate as a free-standing entity. "There will be no direct relationship between the stores. But the affiliation will give us increased merchandising ability. Denholms is stronger in most departments than we are, and we can take advantage of that,"[17] stated Johnson.

News of the merger was documented in the local newspapers, the *New York Times* and the many retail trade newspapers. As part of the merger, Corsini and Feist were interviewed by the local media about the future of Denholms. All reassurances were made to the public that they would not see any visible changes to the Denholms organization and that the store was still maintaining healthy profits, allowing for future growth. The merger was viewed as a positive step forward for the nearly 100-year-old company, and discussions revolved around the new Auburn store as well as the plans for the 100th anniversary celebration.

In preparation for the new Auburn opening, Corsini made the decision to revamp the Denholms logo, which would be used on the new store signage as well as the shopping bags and boxes that would service the two stores. The new design was a collaboration between the advertising department and the display department, which was now headed up by Bob Branczyk after Eric Hallback left Denholms to pursue other opportunities. The updated logo was designed in a bold calligrapher's

The Denholms' updated shopping box, featuring gold and white stripes.

A Denholms delivery truck, 1970.

The new Denholms logo.

freehand style and placed on a new backdrop of gold and white stripes. The new signage was also incorporated onto the downtown Worcester store in the form of a six-foot-wide backlit sign placed above the 484 entrance to the building. In an effort to continue the branding efforts of the new design, the gold and white stripes were used as prop backdrops for various in-store displays and newspaper advertisements, as well as on a new fleet of delivery trucks.

With the Auburn store beginning to take shape, another Corsini entered the retail scene. Frank Corsini, one of Russell's five sons, came on board to manage the new Auburn store. Frank was a graduate of Clark University and was interested in the field of retail. Having grown up with the store as a major part of his life, he understood the culture and principles behind the Denholm name. All efforts were made to allow him to be fully incorporated into the Denholms environment. Partnering with the various buyers and merchandise managers, he traveled to New York on buying trips to assist with the opening of the new store. As a young, intelligent and personable man, Frank was well suited to manage the new store at the high levels of service and standards that Denholms was founded on.

Frank Corsini.

Opening Day

On March 23, 1970, the new Auburn store opened for its first day of business. The new store was designed with an open concept configuration, with few interior walls breaking up the space, and was clad in a dark brown glazed brick on the exterior, with the new Denholms font placed above all three entrances as backlit signage. The Auburn store was two stories high and occupied ninety-six thousand square feet of selling space. The popular boutiques, such as the Salisbury Shop, the Varsity Shop and the millinery department, were incorporated into the new design and laid out in the respective departments. The interior of the store featured most of the departments found in the downtown Worcester store and was fashioned with the escalators as a central form of access to the store's second floor. The interior décor was composed of stainless steel bands boxing in hanging globe lights anchored over the jewelry, accessory and

The new Denholms Auburn store.

cosmetic departments. Colorful wall coverings of deep red and gold papered the walls of the men's clothing department, while softer hues of green and lilac anchored the women's departments. A new juniors Mod Shop was designed with New York's Studio 54 as its inspiration. Floating walls of chrome and frosted glass were suspended from the ceiling, with large studio lights spotlighting the merchandise, which was housed in simple chrome cube fixtures. A disc jockey was on hand to spin records to further add to the youthful environment.

In anticipation of the opening, shoppers eagerly gathered outside the store's entrances, forming massive crowds. The *Worcester Telegram* was on hand to photograph the crowds outside as well as the first shopper who entered into the store. The inaugural customer was photographed for a newspaper article alongside Russell Corsini, who draped a cashmere coat over her shoulders for the press pictures. To help create a festive environment for the opening celebration, an informal fashion show was held in the new Mod Shop, where customers could view the latest in fashion, from the popular maxi dresses to the more casual hippie-inspired designs. For the time being, management felt that it had made the right decision in opening the Auburn store. Times were changing, and Denholms was attempting to service the new suburban customer base and grow the corporation outside of its Worcester store, which now gained flagship standing.

A CELEBRATION

In previous years, Denholms had always focused its large spring and fall promotions on various countries as a main theme. But this year was a special one. The store had now been in business for one hundred years, and Russell Corsini decided to pay homage to the company's history over that time span. A new shopping bag of vivid pink with black silhouettes of women from the late 1800s to the modern day was designed as a special tribute to the store's heritage and used in the ladies' third-floor sportswear and dress departments only. On the store's fifth floor, a retrospective of the store was on display for the viewing public. Shoppers could glance at

Women's shopping bags for the 100th anniversary.

rare photographs of the early store on Mechanics Street alongside images of the first fleet of delivery trucks used to transport shoppers' purchases. The archive also contained imagery from early fashion shows, the façade change in 1951 and rare photographs of William Alexander Denholm and William C. McKay. Along the store's Main Street windows, modern fashions of the day including chiffon pantsuits for women, evening gowns and accessories displayed in front of the new signature gold and white stripes, which wrapped the perimeter walls of the windows as a backdrop. The signage "Denholms 100 Years Young" was applied to the walls in a high-gloss Lucite and carried through the store's thirteen windows, including those on High Street.

The anniversary celebration continued through the Christmas season, when another specially designed shopping bag illustrated the company's major milestones, starting with the first store on Mechanics Street in 1870, followed by the new Main Street store in 1882, the façade change in 1951 and the new Auburn store in 1970. For the exterior holiday trim on the Worcester building, Corsini decided to abandon the large tree of lights that had graced the building every year since 1955, as its wiring was starting to wear out. To commemorate the 100th anniversary

Denholms' new exterior Christmas trim, 1970.

and continue with a Denholms tradition, a new design concept of three smaller lit trees was placed on the building's façade above the marquee to give the store a more updated image. The smaller trees gave a more understated appeal to the structure while still heralding the Christmas season and enchanting young children.

Chapter 14
A Changed Downtown

By the late spring of 1971, the downtown Worcester store had received a thorough power wash and cleaning in preparation for the new shopping center to open. The façade had not had a deep cleaning since it was unveiled in 1951, and Denholms wanted to put its best foot forward for the new tenants. Russell Corsini knew that the new mall would affect the Denholms operations in Worcester and had planned for the flagship store to take a 25 percent drop in business. In 1971, the downtown Worcester store averaged $12 million in sales, and the new Auburn branch took in $4 million for its opening year.

On July 29, 1971, the new Worcester Center Galleria opened for business. Large crowds of people fled to the new mall to get their first glance at downtown Worcester's largest construction project and to shop the new assemblage of stores. The mall at the time was one of the finest examples of a downtown-area indoor shopping center and had been compared to the Galleria Vittorio Emanuele in Milan. The opening festivities included music, performances and special sales and promotions. Throughout the year, Russell Corsini and the upper management of the store tracked the sales of their downtown operation closely and were relieved when the first-quarter results showed sales consistent with their expectations. During a newspaper interview, Corsini announced that in order to further compete with the new mall and maintain Denholms' position in the marketplace, a decision had been made to purchase the abutting Richard Healy Building. Richard Healy had been vacant for eight months after a ninety-year run in the city. The store had specialized in upscale furs and women's apparel. Due to declining sales and the changing demographics of the downtown area, a decision was made to close the store and sell the real estate, which had been purchased by the Healy Company in 1948. Floor plans for the Healy space had not yet been finalized, as Denholms first needed to break through its abutting wall and join together the two spaces, which were at differing elevations.

At the same time that the newspapers were covering the expansion project, Corsini announced that he planned to retire in September 1971 but would stay on in a consultant capacity, as well as his continued position as the executive vice-president over the Denkay Corp. Howard Feist would succeed Corsini as president of Denholms, and Fred Cooper of East Greenwich, Rhode Island, would be named executive vice-president. Cooper was a native of Paterson, New Jersey, and had graduated from Rutgers University. His lengthy background in the retail world consisted of thirteen years of management experience with the Allied Stores Corporation, two years as merchandising manager for Miller & Rhoads out of Richmond and a position as executive vice-president for the Cleland-Simpson Company, which was based out of Scranton, Pennsylvania. In 1970, Cooper had moved to Rhode Island, where he joined the Feist group as executive vice-president of the Shepard's stores, as well as the newly acquired Gladding's stores, which were also based in Rhode Island.

During an interview with Fred Cooper, it was also announced that Frank Corsini would be leaving the Auburn store coinciding with his father's retirement plans. "He's 24 years old, bright, and smart; he's top notch, and I'm sure he has definite plans for his future," stated Cooper. He also affirmed that Denholms had experienced some financial difficulties lately but "we were not disappointed when it did occur." He went on to say, "In this total corporation, there is no lack of money, and we intend to get Denholms back to where it was formerly. We do not view it as a stress situation, we are merchants, and we are here to stay."[18] As part of the restructuring of management, John McLoughlin was named vice-president and general manager over the downtown Worcester and

Auburn stores. McLoughlin had been with Denholms for over sixteen years and had most recently held the title of merchandise manager over all the hard line areas of the store.

HEALY BUILDING

By March 1972, Denholms had acquired the Healy store and made the necessary interior renovations to house a new discount operation under the Denholms name. The new space was stocked mostly with manufacturers' overruns of women's and men's clothing, small appliances and lower-priced furniture and appliances. The new management was hoping to capitalize on the growing trend of "off-price" retailers that were springing up in downtown and suburban areas throughout the nation. The discount concept was new for Denholms, as the store had been known for quality goods that were sold at suggested retail prices dictated by the manufacturers. The hope was that the new discount annex would add an incremental volume in sales to the main flagship store. John McLoughlin took ownership over the new annex and worked directly with the vendors to get below-market prices by purchasing large volumes of goods to sell. While the annex was still in its infancy stage, the main full-price store was starting to gain momentum again as the novelty of the Worcester Center was slowing down and regular customers were returning to Denholms to shop.

The Main Street shopping district was changing. Storefronts were now lying vacant from the relocation to the new shopping center or filled with smaller, less attractive startup businesses. The crowds that used to dominate the downtown-area streets now shifted to the indoor Galleria or smaller outlying malls. Worcester was not alone in the shift toward suburban malls or the decline of the downtown area. Many cities across the country were facing the same dilemma and struggled to keep their main streets vibrant. The management at Denholms continued to focus on the current business trends both locally and nationally to adapt to the changing times.

Partnering with the City of Worcester, a decision was made to hold an event to get shoppers back to Main Street. The city decided to hold a large parade of floats, in which Denholms would be the main attraction. Russell Corsini, who was still active with the company on a consulting level, partnered with Bob Branczyk and the advertising department to come up with a theme for the event. In the past, Denholms had kept most of its promotions in store, other than the fashion shows that were held for various charities throughout the city. The downtown event needed to be a spectacle to help revive the once thriving area. The approved theme was a retrospective of fashions from the 1700s to present-day 1972, appropriately named a Parade of Fashions. The display department constructed a float consisting of sixteen thousand California straw flowers, which covered a wire form of an early Victorian woman. The statue alone was twenty-five feet high and was positioned on a large flatbed covered in boxwood and additional straw flowers. On the float, poised alongside the statuette, were live models donned in period clothing from the different eras of American history. In preparation for the float to move down Main Street, the city removed low-hanging cables and streetlamps that might interfere with the statue as it made its way down the avenue. Once again, the streets of Worcester were packed with onlookers to see the float and take in the festivities. The crowds of people were reminiscent of what was now becoming a bygone era.

Chapter 15
The Shutters Go Up

At the beginning of 1973, the Denholm and McKay Company started to regain its financial strength and acquired the adjoining S.S. Kresge store that abutted the building. Howard Feist purchased the space through the Denholms Corporation under the Mayflower Properties Trust for $690,000—far over the assessed price of $400,000. S.S. Kresge had long been an institution on Main Street until it closed on December 31, 1972. At that time, Kresge sublet the vacant space to American Discount Stores, which was based in New Haven, Connecticut. The new occupant's lease would run until December 31, 1974, and at that time, Denholms would take full possession of the building to further expand. "This action completes our acquisition of properties in this area and now we can start planning for further expansion in conjunction with the Worcester Plaza Development,"[19] Feist stated. The extension that was planned for Denholms would enable the retailer to have full possession of all real estate from Chatham Street to Barton Place, which ran alongside the former Kresge building.

On the surface, all appeared well at Denholms. The store was obtaining new real estate, and sales in both the Auburn and Worcester stores were meeting their monthly financial plans. On the inside, product assortments within the two stores were starting to make a more dramatic shift from full-price retail to more off-price, lower-end goods. Feist, who also owned the moderately priced Darling Knitwear, began selling merchandise to

Denholms for full retail; these items would be resold to the public at off price, thus eroding the profit margins. Large sale tables were now filling the sprawling aisles within the store to house the new discount items from Feist-owned companies. The buyers and executives began to field complaints from customers and sales associates about the cheaper assortment of merchandise being carried at both stores. The allocated dollars that each buyer was given to purchase seasonally was also starting to shrink as Feist was holding controlling reins over all financials within his organizations.

At the same time in Rhode Island, both Shepard's and Gladding's were going through tough financial times inside their conglomerates. Both stores were suffering from a drop in sales and poor management over their internal financial operations. As part of a hastily planned solution, Howard Feist withdrew funds from Denholms accounts to help keep his failing stores afloat. This withdrawal of finances had devastating effects on the business within the coming months. During the retailer's 103-year history, all merchandise purchased for the store had been paid in full by cash funds. Without the cash on hand, vendors and all store line expenses were not being paid. During several follow-up orders to replenish stock that had sold through, the buyers of the store were told that no merchandise would be sent until payment had been made. Even the store's best vendors were not allowing orders or selling on credit until Denholms' status in the marketplace turned around. Several complaints were fielded to Feist, who assured the store that all invoices would be paid in full and in a timely manner. During the whole ordeal, correspondence was made by the buyers and managers to Corsini with hopes that he could rectify the problem, but there was nothing he could do; his present role did not allow him to control the business or finances outside of his consulting role. Feist was using the store as a virtual bank to support his other interests, and Denholms was starting to suffer the consequences.

In an effort to offset the deficit, Feist and Cooper made the decision to lay off employees and cut the payroll. The Auburn store, which had been in business for nearly two years and opened with 200 employees, was now reduced by half. The flagship Worcester store, which would normally staff 600 employees at Christmastime and 450 year round, was reduced to 300. The layoffs were done by seniority in both stores, and the process took a full week, during which associates feared for their jobs after viewing other employees being told that they were no longer needed. The layoffs affected all levels within the organization, from management and buyers down to the associates and support personnel. The mood in the store was somber as associates said goodbye to longtime colleagues while fearing for their own jobs.

On September 14, 1973, the Denholm and McKay Company, as well as Shepard's and Gladding's, was sold by Feist, who was suffering through a financial breakdown. This was the second time in four years that Denholms had been sold to a new parent company. The sale was made to Eastern Dry Goods, which was a New York holding company, and included the inventory, stock in trade and the business name of the company at both its Worcester and Auburn stores. The Main Street building, along with the former Richard Healy space, was obtained by the Denkay Corporation, which held the first mortgage on the real estate, while the Auburn store remained as a leased space (held by Denkay) through the mall.[20] Eastern Dry Goods had only been incorporated for three months and had been started up by Maurice Olen. Olen had been in the process of buying up financially troubled stores with plans to liquidate or sell them off as a going business. Once considered a "boy wonder" of retail, Olen's past included building a chain of 125 stores know as the Olen Stores before he was thirty-five years old. The stores later merged with H.L. Green Company, and Olen became the chief executive of both companies. Following this, another merger was made by Olen between the H.L. Green Company and the McCrory-McLellan stores. Before the amalgamation of the two companies took place, a $3 million deficiency in inventory was found at the Green Company. This forced Olen to resign.[21] As part of the court order, Olen was placed on a five-year probation, which lasted through 1975. One of the conditions of the probation was that Olen would not accept any funds for investment or receive any fees or commissions of any kind. News of the sale and probation circulated throughout the Worcester and New York papers and caused great unease within the Denholms stores.

Before the ink could dry on the sale, a new blow to Denholms took place. Three creditors who were still awaiting payment from Denholms filed a suit in Boston District Court announcing involuntary bankruptcy against the store. The total debt owed by Denholms reached $250,000 and represented claims from over 150 creditors who urged the court to take control over the company's assets and supervise a liquidation of the store. Both the Shepard's and Gladding's stores were closed overnight as a separate claim of $1.25 million was filed against Shepard's as a result of nonpayment on a loan Feist had taken out on the store. In reaction to the unfavorable press that was surrounding the Feist-owned stores, the fur department at Denholms (which was a leased operation) was blocked off by Worcester police and the store executives due to threats that the owner of the furs wanted to remove his inventory and vacate the premises. As part of the lease agreement, no merchandise could be extracted without approval from the Denholms officials.[22] Rumblings of a closing were starting to make their way throughout the store, creating further unease. John McLoughlin tried to assure associates that the store would remain open for business as usual, but no one knew for sure what the future held for the Denholm and McKay Company.

Worcester Closes

Eastern Dry Goods and Maurice Olen had been closely watched by the courts and the probation officers, and a determination was made that Olen needed to sell his stock in Denholms to avoid further prosecution. To appease the courts, Eastern Dry Goods sold the common stock to Worcester Properties, Inc., giving that company control over the business. They hoped to reorganize with a loan of $200,000 from the Worcester County National Bank. The loan was used to plump up formerly empty racks and counters and instill a sense of confidence in the two stores. The sense of security would be short-lived, as First Hartford Realty, which owned the Auburn mall, filed suit to evict Denholms for failure to pay back rent, failure to maintain an adequate stock of merchandise and failure to pay its share of 1973 real estate taxes.[23]

In an effort to pacify the courts under the bankruptcy protection, a determination was made to liquidate the Worcester store and try to make a last stand in Auburn. John McLoughlin held an all-store meeting on November 6 and announced that the Worcester store would be closing on November 16 and all efforts would be placed into the Auburn store. Shock and disbelief spread throughout the store. Even though news of a closing had made its way into the papers, associates were still in denial that the once grand store would be closing. McLoughlin tried to calm the crowd and assured that they would take on as many associates as they could in the Auburn location.

To prepare for the closing, trucks arrived at the Worcester store and began clearing full-price merchandise to bring to Auburn, leaving sections of the store empty. Departments such as infants and juniors were now being consolidated into the former dress department as the size of the store started to shrink. On the fourth floor, the former furniture department was stripped bare except for a few lonely mattresses leaning up against supporting columns. The main-floor cosmetic cases were now empty and used to hold a variety of goods from epicure to wallets, as well as scarves, all being separated by price point. Throughout the building, the display department was hard at work removing departmental signage, props and mannequins to make way for additional sale tables to house consolidated departments. The Main Street windows were stripped of all merchandise, and large "going out of business" signs were strung from the ceiling.

The store held a 30-percent-off liquidation sale of all remaining product, excluding the sale of fixtures, as the fate of the building was still undetermined. On November 16, large crowds of customers filled the store, picking through the final remnants of sale product to get one last look at the former "Boston Store." "It's so empty now," said a first-floor sales clerk. "In the past there'd be Christmas decorations all over the place, and more stock coming in. Everyone would be so busy. It's just so sad today." Another former manager at the store simply stated, "The name was magic; there will never be another Denholms."[24] Besides looking for bargains, several customers made their way to the store to pass along their condolences to the associates they had grown to know. Some offered hugs and well wishes, and others offered a shoulder to cry on. The store's display windows were now bare of signage, and case lines were assembled to block off upper levels of the vacant store. With

Denholms on Main Street, circa 1973.

the sale winding down and six o'clock approaching, the final shoppers made their way outside into a cold November night, followed by the store managers, who swiftly locked the doors behind them. All that was left now of the former "Boston Store" was a big empty building on Worcester's Main Street.

After the Worcester store closed, Denholms set up shuttle buses that took customers from the former Worcester location to the Auburn store. The buses would run every hour on the hour and would assist customers who didn't have cars to still do their Christmas shopping with Denholms. As a form of goodwill toward the remaining stores along Main Street, Russell Corsini stepped in and had the vacant Worcester store's windows dressed for the holidays using the former animatronic window displays. Corsini did not want existing retailers to suffer from the loss of Denholms.

With sadness in the air, the Auburn store coasted through the Christmas season, but the realities of the financial impacts were evident. The store owed back taxes and rent on the two locations, as well as the loan that had been taken out during the reorganization process. The sales that would be generated by the single Auburn store could not offset its debts, and the decision was made to close. During a newspaper interview, the receiver in bankruptcy for the store declared, "For all intents and purposes, the Denholm and McKay Company is dead...The store will close on January 14th."[25]

In an effort to pay off back taxes and rent to the Auburn location, an agreement was made with First Hartford Realty to purchase all the fixtures at the remaining Auburn store and allow the store to vacate the premises. With the announcement of the closing made public, the Auburn store held its liquidation sale. In order to expedite the process, a more generous discount of 40 percent was made on all merchandise. When the sale was advertised in the paper, crowds of shoppers fled to the store to purchase their final items from Denholms. Auburn police were on hand to create an order of assembly in the parking lot, as the onslaught of cars was backing up roadways and intersections. Inside the store, shoppers were running up the down escalators in search of deals in the second floor's electronics department, while ladies were abandoning dressing rooms and simply trying on clothes in the middle of the sales floor, to the dismay of store executives.

On January 14, during its last day of business, associates were grieving the loss of a company that once stood so proud and reminisced with customers about their days with Denholms. As closing time approached and a few stragglers were still walking about the empty store looking for last-minute bargains, a tearful voice came over the loudspeaker: "It is now nine o'clock, and Denholms is closed." It was a final reminder that the days of shopping with the Denholm and McKay Company were officially over.

At the time of the Auburn store's closing, a lawsuit was made by the trustees of Denholms against Howard Feist. The suit claimed that he had unlawfully diverted Denholms' assets to other Feist-controlled businesses and himself. The claims charged that Denholms went into insolvency and bankruptcy due to Feist's mismanagement of funds and stated that he had bought up Denholms investment stock for far under market value. As the daily newspapers covered the rise and fall of Denholms and tracked the legal allegations against the former owner, Feist went into seclusion and refused any interviews.

A FINAL SALE

In April 1975, one final sale took place at the former Worcester location. To satisfy the remainder of debt owed to the banks, an auction was held to sell off the remaining fixtures. The sale was held by Richard Corsini (Russell's son), who was now in charge of the former store's real estate. A crowd of customers, local shop owners and citizens longing to get one last look at the former store arrived to purchase a piece of memorabilia. As the auctioneer walked about the store with a megaphone, attendees perused the various props and fixtures that had remained in the store after the closing. The shopping bags that once filled the Worcester streets sold for one dollar per thousand, and the large Persian rug that graced the first floor was cut up and sold by the yard. In a corner by the former fur salon sat Santa's chair next to a host of other memories. As Richard walked through the empty store and passed by the former beauty salon, the now empty Salisbury Shop and the former men's suits department, he picked up a picture of the former delivery trucks and saved it for memory's sake. "Some of the older people still call it the Boston Store," he stated, and then fondly reminisced about Denholms' golden years.[26]

At the end of 1973, the *Worcester Telegram and Gazette* voted the closing of Denholms to be the second most newsworthy event behind the Watergate hearings. Over the next few years, articles concerning the former store and the impact it left on Main Street still entered into the daily news as former associates and customers wrote in to comment on their favorite Denholms recollections. While the once great store was gone, it would forever live on as a symbol of a kinder, grander era of retailing.

The Denholm building lay vacant and was owned by the city for ten years, with various proposals to use the space as an apartment building or government offices or to level the building to make room for expanded parking. In 1983, a development firm out of Boston named Craig Heath Associates took on the project of resurrecting the former department store into office condominiums on the upper floors, with the main floor segregated into smaller retail shops and a café. The most notable change would be to the exterior of the building, where the narrow bands of windows that had existed were changed out for larger bronze panes to

The Denholms building, present day.

allow more light to enter into the building. The small Denholm and McKay signage that perched on top of the marquee was discarded, and a new Denholms sign was affixed to the building as a formal reminder of the store that once resided there. The new façade was modeled after the computer-based office towers that dotted Route 9. The local papers ran stories about the building's many exterior transformations over the years, highlighting its original appearance in 1882, the façade change in 1951 and its present-day appearance. The interior of the building was also refurbished and subdivided into separate office condominiums from 1,500 square feet and up on all floors to fill the space. It wasn't long before several nonprofit organizations and law offices took up residency within the converted structure and made their own modifications to the former store to suit their needs. The building that Clark designed in 1882 had gone through many incarnations and was now repurposed back to its original plan. As people still file in on a daily basis to conduct business, many refer to the building as a Worcester landmark and are more than happy to recollect on their days spent at Denholms.

Epilogue

What started out as a small business endeavor between two men grew to become Worcester's largest and most modern department store. The dedication of numerous talented and loyal individuals helped propel the store through its most prosperous years—a bygone era when men and women still donned their finest apparel to go downtown and do their shopping. With its various promotions, the store allowed customers to partake in fantastic visual journeys to faraway lands, all while shopping for their latest Denholms purchase. It was a simpler time when the city was overflowing with residents who would flock to the store just to view the large illuminated tree and peruse the magnificent window displays. Like many downtown retailers of the past, Denholms was not alone in succumbing to the changing face of retail. The rise of suburbia and the need for purchasing goods at discount prices eventually led to their downfall. Today, the historic Denholm Building still stands. Gone are the gold and white shopping bags, the perfectly styled mannequins and the festive holiday displays. But there are still glimpses of its retail heyday. The exterior marquee, hand-gilded escalators and revolving doors on the first floor are a silent reminder that the once grande dame of Main Street held reign over a city she loved.

Memoirs by Pat Wolf

ACKNOWLEDGEMENTS AND DEDICATION

I would like to acknowledge all who contributed to my quest for memories about Denholms, especially my sisters, Amy, Diana, Alice and Pamela, and my brothers, Harry Jr., John and Tony.

Special thanks are in order for my cousin Richard H. Kearns, who worked at Denholms in the summer of 1961 and supplied memories, photographs and genealogy; for my niece Katherine C. Brazauskas, who provided encouragement, research and drafts; and my niece Jennifer R. Traub, who assisted me in the editing process.

I owe all that I have written to my parents, Harry F. Wolf and Alice Constant Francis Wolf, whose guiding principles—do your best, be fair and make a personal connection—have served me well.

I would like to dedicate this book to all who made Denholms possible, especially Josephine Carbone, whose love and passion for life and Denholms was so strong and deep that her young grandson, Christopher Sawyer, inherited her love and passion, and as a result, Denholms has been brought back to life.

My father, Harry Florian Wolf, was born on Easter Sunday, and as one of his tennis friends wrote, "He always seemed to embody the optimism and spirit of this joyous day," which fell on March 31 in the year 1907.

He was the eldest of four children born to Crescentia Bertha née Schmitt and Henry Wolf, who lived in the Bronx. Harry's father was born in New York City in 1870, went to college in Ohio and went on to become one of the leaders in the business world. Long identified with the retail business, Henry Wolf was treasurer of Denholm and McKay Company and was also treasurer and one of the founders of the Novelty Handkerchief Manufacturing Company of New York City and Passaic, New Jersey. For forty years, Henry Wolf worked for the Syndicate Trading Company, a resident buying office, and also became treasurer of the same. He also was president of Almy's Limited, a department store in Montreal, Canada.

"Success lies in mutual service. The way to success is to keep faith with every customer and make each one a friend." This was the underlying principle of Almy's, Montreal's largest department store, as expressed by Mr. Wolf. Harry went to grammar school and then on to St. Peter's Preparatory High School in Newark, New Jersey. He matriculated at Williams College, Williamstown, Massachusetts, and graduated Phi Beta Kappa in 1929. He wore out several pairs of shoes looking for work in New York City and found his first job working for the Equitable Trust Company. Later on, he joined his father at the Novelty Handkerchief Company in Passaic, New Jersey, as treasurer and general manager. He married Alice Francis, a top tennis player, in 1934. By 1942, with a family of four children, my father was sent to Worcester, Massachusetts, by his father to become the general manager of Denholm and McKay Company.

In a letter dated August 1, 1943, Bill Farrington, who was stationed at Fort Eustis and became the buyer for the men's department at Denholms, wrote, "I believe you would like this training, Harry, as everything is very exact—timing to the second and systemized to perfection. The army accepts no excuses for carelessness and continually keeps us 'on the ball.' You are very exacting in your work and carry out every detail so well that you would get quite a 'kick' out of it."

The April 13, 1944 edition of the *Worcester Daily Telegram*[27] reported on a dinner dance and entertainment that was given by the Denholms' management for over four hundred people attended by Mr. Krim, the Corsinis and my parents, when my father was vice-president and general manager. In the 1946 winter publication of *Switchboard*,[28] it reported that he "gives his personal supervision to telephone service in order to make certain that telephone contacts are handled by his employees in a courteous helpful manner." In September 1946, he was elected president, and dozens of congratulatory letters are a testament to his popularity.

DENHOLMS

As far back as I can remember, and even further back than I can remember, Denholms has been part of my life. I have photos showing me welcoming the Easter bunny on Main Street with a group of young cheerleaders. Another shows me offering a bouquet of carrots to the Easter bunny. I don't remember these specific events, but I remember being at home at Denholms. I am the seventh of eight children born to my parents, who moved to Shrewsbury when my father was sent to become the general manager of Denholms in 1942. We were enrolled in St. Paul's Cathedral Elementary School, which was kitty-corner to the High Street entrance to Denholms. This afforded us children the opportunity to see where our father worked each school day. When there were five or six of us, our mother packed a lunch of sandwiches with thermos bottles of milk, and we would eat in one of the stockrooms on the third floor. After school, my mother would pick us up, and frequently, she would do some shopping. This gave us a chance to see the merchandise and lobby to buy something. The highlight of every year was the visit to Santa, with an accompanying photo taken by Marvin Richmond. I have Santa photos of each of my siblings, and inevitably anyone who shopped at Denholms had their Santa photos also. In the spring, Easter afforded more photos taken with the Easter bunny. Near the camera stand were real live rabbits, Flopsy, Mopsy and Cottontail. After the holiday, Flopsy, Mopsy and Cottontail sometimes found their way to our house, where they lived in a hutch.

I would describe Denholms as a combination of Disneyland, a shopping adventure and a community center. The customer was always right, and one would hear the refrain, "Meet me at Denholms." Service with a smile was the policy; in fact, my father used to hand out small cards that said "Keep Smiling." When the older children went to high school,

I ate lunch with my father in his office on the fifth floor, and before I returned to school, there was enough time for a game of gin rummy or cribbage. On some occasions, my father gave me the task of putting checks through his check-writing machine that would put his signature on the appropriate line. All this needed to be recorded with the beginning and ending check numbers and date.

I remember exactly what was in his office and the two buttons on the back credenza that allowed him to buzz people into the office from the outside door and to summon Lucy, his secretary. Adjacent to my father's office was Lucy's office. She was a longtime employee whose loyalty and service were second to none. My brother John remembers her as the nicest person. "She was also very kind to type my grammar school papers." Lucy was loyal, hardworking and very personable. When requested, she would accompany us children to the bus and wait until we boarded before returning to the store. Lucy's office was narrow, with the usual office furniture and equipment, but the one I remember the most was the mimeograph machine with blue typed master and the smell of the fluid that made the copies. It probably was not healthy, but I distinctly remember the smell and the rhythm of the copies being churned out one at a time. Lucy's sister, Sabina, was a saleslady in the notions department on the main floor. Outside of these two offices was a desk where Eileen Taymens sat. I seem to remember she had an accent, and I would guess that she might have been British. She had toffee candies wrapped in paper on her desk. After her departure, Mary Loach took on the post of receptionist and secretary for Russell Corsini, the merchandising manager, whose office was adjacent to Lucy's. Across from Eileen's desk was a mailbox area for the buyers with about fifty cubbyholes, each labeled alphabetically: Beach, Berliner, Carbone…

One particular department I liked was the gift wrap desk on the second floor. We spent much time there, especially when my mother did Christmas shopping. I don't remember the woman's name, but I remember studying her technique. After cutting the selected paper to the needed size, she folded, creased and taped with amazing dexterity and accuracy. Then the ribbon and bow, swish, turn, flair, fluff and voila—a perfect gift perfectly wrapped. Another favorite department on the main floor was the candy department and gourmet shop managed by Dot Eagen, of average height, blonde hair and a ready smile. S.S. Pierce delicacies in their fancy red cans and British warrant were considered a treat and were more expensive than their American counterparts. Russell Stover candies were sold exclusively at Denholms in boxes of milk chocolates, dark chocolates, pastel-colored candies and the box that offered more choices: Little Ambassadors. Upon opening the box, a sheet of paper folded neatly over the nestled chocolates identified the contents of each candy. Just around the corner was one of the lease departments, eyeglasses, manned by A. Goral. This was a small area, but it afforded Mr. Goral the chance to benefit from all the foot traffic on the main floor, and in return, he paid to rent that space from Denholms.

Personal service epitomized the shopping experience at Denholms. Mabel Finney, head of the stationery and card department, received a note in 1965 from the Kem Plastic Playing Cards Company, whose policy was to replace damaged cards with the matching design. "Your request for a replacement has been forwarded to us, and it is our pleasure to be of service. The three of diamonds has been replaced and we trust Mr. Wolf will now find his Kem Cards satisfactory in every respect." To the right of the elevators on the north side was the children's shoe department, which Mr. Berliner managed. He was not quite Mr. Rogers, but he had a way with kids. Stride-Rite was the brand of choice, and the sneakers were PF Flyers. Of course, there were those standard foot-measuring devices where you placed your heel in one end and then a sliding piece at the side measured the width of your foot. And then there was this kind of X-ray machine in which you would place your feet and look down through a scope and see your feet in a sea of florescent green. I think it was used to look at the bones of the foot. From there, one could head through the men's department, headed by Bill Farrington, and take the staircase to the left of the three elevators on the south side down to the lower level.

There on the right, at the foot of the stairs, was the bakery, run by Mrs. Jaffe. Two or three large display cases kept the daily cupcakes, cakes and pastries fresh. I especially liked the chocolate frosting on the white cupcakes with the paper all around. In later years, a restaurant was set up on the lower level. The food was good at a reasonable price.

The menu for Tuesday, November 20, 1962, included: roast leg of spring lamb, dressing, mint jelly, whipped potatoes, natural gravy and buttered green peas, all of which was served with a roll and butter, all for $1.35. The minimum table charge was $0.35 per person from 11:00 a.m. to 3:30 p.m.

Housewares were sold in one section of the lower level, and around the corner was the shoe repair, the big walk-in safe and, at one point, the toy department. On special occasions, a Lionel train track was set up to run through tunnels and up hills. Every boy and some girls wanted a Lionel train set for Christmas. Lionel even offered a girls' train in 1957, with a pink locomotive and tender and pastel-colored freight cars. I even remember a life-size locomotive cab with whistle; it may have been from Chesapeake and Ohio, their mascot being Chessie, the sleeping cat. Eventually, the toy department moved to the third floor when the High Street addition was built. The buyer's name was Ann Coggins; she had white-gray hair, glasses and a deep voice. This was a popular place to visit all year round.

Also ensconced on the lower level were shoe repair and an entrance to a freight elevator. Beside the shoe repair was a big walk-in vault where cash and other valuables could be secured. Once, some men hid in the store after closing hours. They went to this vault, broke in and made off with the contents. After that, my father had ADT or a similar alarm installed so that this unfortunate situation would not happen again.

The record department was managed by Miss Midge Beach, a thin lady of average height with curly brown hair. It was located on the fifth floor immediately to the left as one stepped out of one of the north-side elevators. Long rows of shelves showcased the latest hits: Frank Sinatra, Bing Crosby, Mitch Miller and the like. And just to make sure the customer got what he wanted, he or she could listen to the recording in one of the soundproof booths before making a purchase. These were the days of 45s, 78s and LPs. One record we purchased by the Inkspots on the Decca label has a Denholms price sticker of sixty-nine cents. Opposite the record department was the luggage department, whose buyer, I think, was Mr. Publicover. Samsonite was a popular brand of the time, and I still have some pieces of it, heavy, sturdy and durable.

Around the corner from the luggage was the camera and film department, managed by Lorraine Sundquist, a young, thin and attractive woman who had a soft manner of speaking. Kodak is the only film I can remember being sold there, as well as cameras. After trips or visits from relatives, during which a lot of pictures would have been taken, the exposed film in its metal container would be dropped off here, and in about a week the photos were ready. Across from cameras was the photography and picture frame department. Professional photography was available, and I can remember at least one photo of myself that was developed there. Beyond the photography was the paint department, and I believe the brand sold there was NU-Tone.

The annex side of the fifth floor was home to the rug department, run by John McLoughlin. Large rolls of carpeting were recessed in the walls, showing their color, style and pile. Lees was a brand that was popular, and there were several with that label in our home. Karastan was another popular brand, advertised in one of the brochures and a window display. It was all wool with oriental patterns but was made by a machine. On the right of the rug department desk was a freight elevator to allow the merchandise to be easily brought to the correct department and, once purchased, to bring the purchase to the shipping department. Continuing toward High Street, on the left was another freight elevator and then the credit department, where Jane Shaw worked. Between credit and payroll were a ladies' room and dumbwaiter that ran up to the sixth floor, where accounting was located. There was also a desk with a phone or two, but I am not sure who worked there. Five women staffed the payroll office: Judy Paciello and Dot Fanning were seated in the back, and three other women sat at the window, one of whom was Nora Londergan. One of Dot's machines was a multiplier with rows and rows of numbers, and when it made a calculation, it would take quite a few seconds before the answer came to rest. Here, people could pay their bills.

Along the westernmost wall was the appliance department, managed by Mrs. Ryan, an older woman of some size. She had gray hair and glasses and seemed to enjoy her role selling washers, dryers and the like. At some point, my father determined that Denholms could not compete with the prices that other stores were able to sell their appliances for, so ultimately, the appliance department closed. The fourth floor was very bright on the south side. Stepping out of one of the elevators, on the right was the china department, whose buyer was Lillian McNeil, who was humorous, had a ready smile and I think was usually chewing gum. The brand of china I remember was Franciscan ware, of which we have the Apple and Desert Rose patterns at home. Glassware was also sold in this department, and I think this is where my oldest sister ordered and purchased Fostoria gold-rimmed goblets as a wedding anniversary present for my parents. Opposite china was the silver department run by Muriel LeClair. There were all kinds of silver dishes, glasses and trays to be seen.

In a little alcove at the top of the stairs, to the extreme left of the south bank elevators, a Trim the Tree Shop was set up for the Christmas season. Lee Porter, a friend of my mother's, worked here for at least a couple of seasons. This was filled with lights, ornaments, artificial trees and the like—a bit of the North Pole in downtown Worcester. On the other side of the fourth floor, near the north-side elevators, was the furniture department. The fondest memory I have of this was the annual tea for the customers. Tea and tea sandwiches made by Julia McGuire were served, while Vanda orchids flown in from Hawaii were handed out to each attendee in a plastic heart-shaped reservoir with a pin that kept the flower stem in water. The sandwiches were so small and delicious that one tended to eat many more than if they were made up as a regular-size sandwich. I believe there were little cupcakes and petit fours. It was special and memorable.

My father drove a cream-colored 1960 Ford Falcon, which he parked in Chase Court running from Chatam Street to Barton Place, an alleyway between the two Denholms buildings. Next to the loading dock was the entrance to the carpenters' workshop. Here Atilio, Vinnie and other skilled carpenters carried out any request that was made of them. I remember the feel of that area with the various tools, varieties of wood and wood products. In an interview with Julie Chase from WTAG, my father extolled the talents these craftsmen demonstrated when they improvised a solution for a quarter-inch gap in the installation of the Escal-Aire. This quick fix made it possible to proceed until the correct fitting was furnished. These gentlemen were always busy remodeling, repairing or creating a new space to keep updating the store.

Another favorite employee was Maurice Zingarelli, a short fellow with a small moustache who was one of the store painters. He followed the completion of the carpenters' work, donned in his painter overalls and hat. He had a methodical and rhythmic energy reflected in his brush strokes. He also seemed to enjoy his work. Also as memorable were the electricians, Mr. Drinkwine and Al Nutter. Mr. Drinkwine was an older gentleman who wore blue overalls and had a shock of white hair and was always on the job. He was the dean of the electrical needs of the store unless the job, was too big in which case, Coghlin Electric Company was engaged. Al Nutter, who was probably half the age of his boss, was a ready, willing and able assistant. Ted Coghlin has said that the large Christmas tree display on the front of the store resulted from my father saying to the crew, "Make it look like Christmas." And what was to appear but twenty strands of lights forming a triangular tree with five thousand shining lights.

In the back of the store before the High Street addition was the shipping area, a large garage that housed five delivery trucks with Denholms advertising on side panels. They backed into a loading dock, from where the trucks were loaded with purchases that required delivery. I think the process went like this: customers who chose to have their purchases delivered or purchases that were too big to carry were brought by freight elevator to the third-floor shipping department. George Corbett, always dressed in a gray jacket similar to what a pharmacist would wear, would process the purchases that would be mailed by parcel post. All other purchases were sent by conveyor belt to the sorting area, headed by Jack Kehoe and his assistant, Budge Dolan. The package would slide down onto a huge steel table. From there, it was placed in a cage and ultimately would be placed in the corresponding truck that delivered to that part of Worcester. The only driver I remember was Frannie. Outside of Mr. Corbett's were two or three vending machines. The one for candy was a maroon color with a mirror above the selections, which only cost a nickel. I think the other machine was for soft drinks. We children appreciated this since sometimes we waited for my mother to finish shopping. In order to make a purchase, we would look for coins under the seat cushions in my mother's car. We inevitably found just what we needed. I remarked on this once, and my brother Tony said he thought my mother may have planted these coins to ensure that our searches would be successful.

The sixth floor was a great place too. The hair salon, managed by Mrs. Dolan, who wore her blonde hair in a French twist, was filled with ladies getting their hair done and maybe manicures, too. There was that distinctive smell that only occurs in hair salons, along with the droning sound of multiple hair dryers and dozens of conversations exceeding the decibels of the dryers. I had my hair cut on some occasions and watched as they swept away my curls into a sea of others' locks. The display department was located on the sixth floor. Here, Eric Hallback, Bob Branczyk, Irving Bostock, Bernice Salmonsen and Dave Socia dazzled the public with their creative, colorful and imaginative posters, displays and themes. I think the one that stands out for me was the time they had canaries in birdcages strategically placed on display cases throughout the main floor in honor of spring. Naturally, the cages were surrounded with floral arrangements, and the canaries sang their songs welcoming the customers and employees alike. My sister Diana remembers a time when a life-sized piper cub airplane was on display on the fifth floor. The mystery was how it was brought into the store. Apparently the wings were removed and the fuselage was transported through a fifth-floor window. The display department was also responsible for decorating the windows on Main Street. These were always refreshed often and enchanted the passersby, who may see something they liked and then become customers. Six albums of pictures capturing the magic of the Denholms display windows were given to me by Eric many years ago for safekeeping. About twenty-five years ago, a young Christopher Sawyer contacted me and asked to borrow some of the photos. He was so excited; he said, "Let's reopen Denholms." His passion and dedication are truly amazing, and I hope he achieves this dream.

The accounting department took up the most space on the sixth floor. Here, twenty or more clerks did all the paperwork. Most memorable among them was Joe Landis, a very short fellow who had previously been a brother in a monastery. He was always smartly dressed and greeted you with a smile. Also on the sixth floor was the advertising department, run by Charlotte Simpson, a tall, artistic lady. She would sketch the skirts, dresses or other merchandise to be sent over to the *Telegram and Gazette* for publication.

The alterations department was in a behind-the-scenes area next to the third-floor windows on Main Street. We had occasion to visit there, and the one seamstress I remember was Helga. Once again, these ladies were skilled and dedicated to the customer and the store. In 1984, about ten years after the store closed, we held a Denholms reunion at our home in Shrewsbury. About 125 people attended. When we served dessert, a large layer cake with the likeness of the front of the store made out of frosting, one of the guests pointed to a window and said, "I have to have that piece. That's where I worked!"

The third floor was probably the most trafficked floor after the main floor. On the north side just after coming up the stairs was the Capezio shop. Here were sold shoes made of Italian leather that had that chic appeal about them. I think just about every young girl had a pair of Capezio flats. To the left of the double bank elevators were women's dresses, neatly displayed on racks among the occasional mannequins. Not far from the Capezios was the area where all the Santa and Easter bunny photos were taken. I remember as a youngster sitting on the lap of the Easter bunny and peering through the mesh of the bunny's eyes and trying to recognize who was inside. Marvin Richmond Studios on Harvard Street was exclusively engaged to photograph these seasonal events. It was a long-standing tradition, and many people still have these photos from their youth.

Around the corner from here was the better dresses department managed by Jo Carbone, Chris Sawyer's grandmother. She imbued her love for the store in her four-year-old grandson, who has single-handedly rekindled the memories of Denholms in person, on the web and in the press. There was something special about Denholms, and that spirit lives on in the minds and hearts of all who shopped there. Far around to the right was the bridal department, run by Elsie McCarthy, a happy, mature woman. On one occasion, my sister Diana organized and emceed a fashion show right in the heart of the third floor. These events

Pat Wolf (center) with
the Denholms Easter
bunny.

generated excitement and were fun. Toward the High Street entrance
was young children's and infants' department headed by Miss Safer, a
stout woman with her sandy brown hair worn in a bun. Carters was
the brand that was prominent for children. Tony Morello was the buyer
for the boys' department, located across from children's. When the High
Street addition was completed in 1961, these departments were able to
offer official Boy and Girl Scout badges and the like.

Keeping an eye on all the activities were floorwalkers Marge O'Connor
on the main floor and my brother John, who met his future bride, Linda
Brousseau, who was working in the candy department. Halfway between
the main and second floors was the office of Mary Loughlin, head of
personnel. A diminutive lady, she was anything but diminutive in taking
charge of the human resources of her day. One of her assistants was
Barbara Falvey. I think there was also a store detective who reported to

Mary. This was an especially busy place before Thanksgiving, as students put in applications to work during the Christmas season. Denholms was also a popular place for young adults to get summer jobs; a priest who attended the party said that was his connection with Denholms. Everyone, it seemed, had worked at Denholms or knew someone who had. People who worked there sometimes met their future spouse, as was the case with my brother John and my sister Pam. Serendipity was involved when Maureen Irish was assigned to fill in at the Santa photo booth one day. She wasn't too anxious to do so, but the young man playing Santa that day, Dennis Irish, became her husband. I worked at Denholms, as did most of my siblings. My experience was assisting on the main floor at the desk where checks were approved. I was pretty young and not that confident, but it was a memorable experience.

My father guided the store through major innovations: air conditioning, the modernization of the façade on the front of the building, the installation of the Escal-Aires and the Chatham and High Street extensions. The planning of the 100th anniversary celebration was still in the planning stages.

But in addition to the customers, the employees and the stockholders was yet another essential group of people who made Denholms possible: the local contractors, including Coghlin Electric Company, Henry Prunier and Sons, Russell Harney Plumbing and Bozenhard Construction. All the men heading these companies that did work at Denholms contributed to the success of the store because of their professionalism, commitment to excellence and skilled craftsmanship. My brother Harry worked on the construction of the High Street extension as an employee of Mr. Bozenhard. Also contributing to Denholms' success was the affiliation with the Mutual Buying Syndicate Incorporated, buyers and consultants to leading department stores. Private brands—such as Selkirk Sportswear, Crib Mates and Baby Set infant wear, Sharon handbags, Mulby housewares, Mor-Flite sporting goods, Lautum linens and domestics and Patty Allen children's sportswear—all were sold exclusively at Denholms. One of Mutual's representatives was a man named Charlie Slater. When he visited Denholms, he was a guest in our home. He loved to talk and ate slowly, so on the occasions when he had to catch a train or plane, my mother was nervous that he would not get there on time.

WTAG INTERVIEW

We learn about the Escal-Aires in a recorded interview with Mr. Wolf and Julie Chase of WTAG:

This is a story of the $100,000 ride. A story written by Denholms to bring better service to the many Denholm customers who will be now enjoying the speed and convenience provided by the new escalators which have just been installed by Denholms.

WTAG: In fact, I have just taken a ride on the escalator, and I think it's about the most glamorous one I have ever seen. You will notice it yourself when you enter Denholms on the street floor. It has sort of a different approach to it, in fact, inspired; the name for the escalator is Escal Aire because it has airiness to it. The actual design going up on either side is made from a silk screening process on plastic sheets which has been pressed between layers of safety glass. It's really gorgeous. This is the most glamorous one I have ever seen, Mr. Wolf.

Wolf: Thank you very much for that description. It actually is a prototype of escalators in New England. And there is only one like it in the United States.

WTAG: Well, as President of Denholms we wanted to ask you a little bit about the background of the escalator. Now, how long ago did you decide this might be something you would like to have in the store?

Wolf: Well, this has actually been a matter of evolution. In respect that over twenty years ago when we first came to Worcester, we realized the facilities of a department store required air conditioning, convenience for vertical transportation and many other facilities which had not been developed up to that time. Consequently, shortly after the war, why we had plans drawn for the installation of an escalator, but the other matters seem to receive prior attention, so this is sort of the belated completion that started a long time ago.

WTAG: Of course as we were riding up on the escalator, we saw many people with us, and they were all so excited to have this available in Denholms now to continue to bring along that feeling that we all have such a nice store in which to shop. How many people could the escalator carry if it had to during a certain period of time?

Wolf: I surely hope we could utilize the full potential of this Escal-Aire installation at least 5,000 people an hour.

WTAG: That would be marvelous, wouldn't it?

Wolf: It sure would!

WTAG: Mr. Wolf, how long ago actually did you start this installation?

Wolf: The actual construction work was begun precisely on the date planned, April the 27th and the installation of the Escal-Aires and the trusses began on the first of June, which followed pretty well on schedule, we are probably just about two weeks behind, but we're glad that it's in operation now.

WTAG: I can imagine though anything of this undertaking, there must have been a few problems and complications you ran into. Any that you can recall?

Wolf: Well, if the contractor had any, I don't know, he didn't tell me. But one thing that I did observe and this is most unusual was that the glass panels finally measured one quarter inch short both in length and width and that's probably the reason why the installation wasn't completed on the date scheduled. Our craftsmen have been sort of ingenious in being able to fit the smaller panels and no one would notice the difference, but to do it right why we'll have the new panels installed at a later date.

WTAG: Of course we have always been impressed by the outstanding selection of merchandise to be found at Denholms and I am sure many people would like to know if installing the Escal-Aires, the escalator, if it's going to take up much of your floor space?

Wolf: Surprisingly not, actually each floor requires about one hundred seventy square feet of space, and by redesigning the fixtures and relocating some of the counters we probably may even effect a more efficient display of our merchandise than we had before.

WTAG: You probably revamp and change things around a little bit, do you think?

Wolf: Yes, naturally the flow of traffic will be different and I would say that the fashion accessory departments on the main floor will be entirely redesigned and refixtured, this is something I would like to do immediately, but, I believe will probably have to be put on the calendar within the next six months.

WTAG: Well, Mr. Wolf, we've been noticing many, of course, progressive steps here at Denholms we are also pleased with the Chatham Annex and I enjoy personally talking about the gourmet shop and visiting it, and budget sportswear and the young third floor and now of course the escalator in operation, could we ask you what is next in store for Denholms besides these things you mentioned about changing perhaps the layout of some of these departments?

Wolf: Well, a glance at the exterior to High and Chatham Street will show that the present YWCA complex is being demolished, we expect that the extended parking area will be available, I hope by the first of October, and that again will provide us with ground level area at the High and Chatham corner of about five to six thousand square feet which will be used for merchandising purposes. Likewise, there are the areas in the YWCA administrative building at the second, third and fourth floor levels that are being studied for merchandising possibilities.

WTAG: I know there is always something more that people would like to do to improve a store and, of course, Denholms seems to be adding to the convenience and enjoyment of their customers. And this seems to indicate to those of us who come into Denholms to shop that you must have a great deal of confidence in downtown Worcester, would you comment on that, Mr. Wolf?

Wolf: Our entire lot is cast in downtown Worcester and we certainly do look forward for the continual improvement of business in the downtown area particularly as the industrial population of our city is increased. This will naturally increase spendable income and I think will be helpful for all the merchants downtown.

WTAG: We would like to thank you very much for talking with us, we have been visiting a Mr. Harry Wolf, the President of Denholms on the occasion of the official opening of the new escalator, the Escal-Aires, and the $100,000 ride. This is a story which has as its happy ending the better service and convenience for the many Denholm customers who enjoy shopping in a really nice store. A story which has been written by a store, Denholms which has shown again the imagination and faith in our downtown area and its future.

DEVOTION

My father died unexpectedly on September 22, 1966. My life went dark, and my world stood still. This came as a great shock to our family, the Denholms employees and the entire community. Jo Carbone and others opened the store for our family to acquire proper attire for the funeral. A picture of my father graced one of the Main Street windows. My mother wrote the following letter to the Denholms employees:

October 1, 1966, To our friends at Denholms, How weak must be the words we use here, and yet, we are trying to express our deep felt appreciation for the kind thoughts, words and actions you have shown over the loss of Mr. Wolf. It is often said that through death, we see life more clearly. It is fitting to say that through you, the living, we have seen more completely the principles and spirit for which Denholms stands. Tragedy does not create these principles and spirit, but it does reflect them through a loyal people such as yourselves. With a grateful voice then, and from the bottom of our hearts, we are saying thank you for your consoling cards, flowers and Mass offerings. We are saying thank you for being you, the life of Denholms. In lasting memory, [Signed] Alice F. Wolf Amy, Harry Jr., Diana, John, Alice, Paul, Patricia, Pamela

Rosemary Fitzgerald wrote:

Dear Mrs. Wolf: I only wish you could have heard the people on the escalators, in the elevators, and everywhere in Denholms. Each one, customer or employee, had some __personal__ recollection of dear Mr. Wolf. People paused before the memorial window too and always they would remark on having seen him somewhere about the store. It was that "daily installment" of good will and kindness and the fact that each of us seemed equally important to Denholms that will keep Mr. Wolf's memory alive in our hearts. Your beautiful letter and your resignation to God's will is a source of inspiration to us all. May God bless you and your family. Sincerely, Rosemary Fitzgerald

The employees commissioned a plaque with a likeness of my father created by Emil Grilli of Shrewsbury. It was placed on the mezzanine between the main and second floor. The officers of Denholms wrote the following:

In Memoriam—Harry F. Wolf, President, Treasurer and General Manager of Denholm & McKay Company died on September 22, 1966, after twenty-four years of devotion to the development of this corporation. A perfectionist in everything he undertook, he dedicated his business life with constructive imagination and rare foresight to enlarging and perfecting the commercial enterprise he headed. At the same time, as a man of many interests, he led a full and active life in which he gave unstintingly of himself to his family, his friends, his flowers, his sports. Scrupulously fair in all his undertakings, he never asked of another any effort he was not prepared to ask doubly of himself. He applied his keen mind, his driving energy and his zeal to excel to every enterprise on which he embarked. He enjoyed the respect and admiration of every person in the organization by the unfailing and lively interest he felt and clearly demonstrated in the well-being of Denholm & McKay Company and every individual involved in its operation. It is therefore, with deep appreciation and a sense of great personal loss that his fellow directors adopt this resolution honoring the devoted service of Harry F. Wolf to this corporation which was so much a part of his life and being. [Signed] Robert S. Bowditch, George R. Harding Jr, Alexander Keyes, and Russell Corsini.

The ensuing years were very difficult. Naturally, we wanted to see Denholms go on, but there was a lack of consensus as to who was in charge and how the store should go on. After Denholms closed, I never went back into the building until recently. It is a shadow of its former grandness, but the personal memories of the good times had by employees and customers alike are indelibly etched in the collective consciousness of all.

In 1973, Dot Fanning's letter to the editor was published:

I feel the need to write these few words regarding the rise and fall of a beautiful Worcester store. For nineteen years, I worked for a wonderful human being, Harry Wolf, president and general manager of Denholm & McKay Co. He worked hard and long to make Denholms the store that it was. It didn't take long for Worcester's famous shopping center to fall flat on its face. Last September 22nd, we attended the seventh anniversary Mass of Mr. Wolf's death. He will be remembered by hundreds of former employees and thousands of customers who enjoyed working and shopping at Denholms. Long live the men of Harry Wolf's caliber. They are few and far, far between.[29]

My sister Amy writes:

My earliest memories of Denholms date back seventy years when I first began to "know" it as a six-year-old child! My father and mother always entered from High Street, which at that time was the "receiving/ shipping/delivery" complex. I could call my father from there (I attended St. Paul's School kitty-corner across the street) by dialing "841" from Mr. Kehoe's phone or dial "operator" to reach the store's own Alice Moynihan, who could reach my mother at home.

This infrastructure, which also included the warren of department back offices, then called "marking rooms," intrigued me then as it does now. Folks (never seen by the "out front" customers) unpacked, inventoried, "priced" and delivered thousands of items to display/ sales areas. I realized over the years that this unseen and unrealized effort underpins what customers observe and take for granted. These memories remain despite that this physical area disappeared with the modernization of the High Street sales expansion/entrance. These early experiences influenced my understanding of economics and history, which I still teach today. My reminiscences of the "old" Denholms (in times when shopping was a more easily understood process) help my students to begin to understand that far more complex and less visible process of 2011.

Recollections

Maureen Irish:

During the late '60s, I was a student at Worcester State College and needed to work part time to earn some money to pay for books and other expenses. I worked at various positions at Denholms during my college years. On one occasion during the pre-Christmas season as I was finishing my shift, the store manager asked me if I would work overtime. This was most unusual. It was the one and only time it happened to me. The manager told me that the photographer for Santa has called in sick at the last minute. I explained that I was not experienced in photography and probably would not take a good picture. She assured me that there was nothing to it and added that I would earn extra money if I helped her out.

I arrived at Santa's location and quickly learned to take the pictures. During the course of the evening, Santa and I chatted and I learned that Santa was also a college student at Clark University. At a break time with his beard off, I realized that Santa was better looking without his disguise. Long story short, we began dating and married two years later. Our first child arrived three years after that on Christmas Eve and we will celebrate our 40th wedding anniversary in July. Thank you Denholms!

My sister Pam met her husband-to-be, Joseph A. Brazauskas, in the men's furnishings department. He was a sales associate, and Pam was a pricing clerk.

My sister Diana worked in the store after college. She learned about retailing, but her specialty was arranging fashion shows at the store and special luncheon shows at the Bancroft Hotel.

Mary Kennedy wrote:

Hanging in the dining room of my family home in Worcester were two portraits of an elderly man and woman. My mother told us they were portraits of our great-grandparents. As a pre-teen in the early 50s, I was

Christmas shopping at Denholms. Imagine my surprise when I walked into the art and frame department at Denholms and found several copies of the same portraits for sale! Gullible me's first thought was: "Good grief! My great-grandparents are famous!" Only later did I discover that these portraits were a popular wedding present in the 1930s and 1940s and were actually entitled "Contented Man" and "Contented Woman" by artist Sidney Bell.

My friend Susan remembers the ride in the elevators and the little jump they made to become level with the floor at which they had stopped. Susan's friend Gina remembers that Denholms was her aunt's favorite store and cherished the bedroom furniture she purchased there. Laurie M. remembers shopping for her Girl Scout badges and using the pay toilets in the second-floor ladies' room. They had green lights that sanitized the seat. When I asked if she crawled under the door, she said, "No, I just waited for someone else to come out and grabbed the door before it closed."

Patricia at the town hall remembers getting all dressed up and accompanying her mother dressed in heels and taking the bus to Worcester to shop at Denholms. She especially remembers having a grilled tuna sandwich in the restaurant. Laura Callahan remembers that as a child, her favorite blanket did a disappearing act; perhaps an adult thought it a bit worn. Laura was distraught, to the point that someone in the neighborhood who worked at Denholms went down to the store and brought back an acceptable duplicate of Laura's security blanket. Cushing Bozenhard, owner of the company that helped construct the High Street extension, recalled telling Mr. Wolf that Mrs. Bozenhard was unable to find a suitable dress for a special occasion. Some time later, while supervising his workmen on the steel beams, Mr. Wolf opened a window in his office on the fifth floor and began waving a dress in Mr. Bozenhard's direction, calling out, "How about this one?"

I remember the pure excitement during the Christmas season. The Christmas crèche was on display in a Main Street window. The Santa photo shop was set up on the third floor. The Christmas tree was aglow on the front of the store. Before December 25, my parents would host a party for the

Santa's chair, circa 1967.

buyers and other executives and their spouses. Cocktails and a buffet dinner were served, and the gift giving followed. Then everyone sang Christmas carols led by Dot Fanning, accompanied by Russ Corsini playing the piano.

Lucy would spend time shopping in the store for gifts for each attendee. In turn, the employees would buy a gift collectively for my parents— oval end tables, beautiful lamps with crystal prisms and the like. Before the party, Eric Hallback and his crew would come out and decorate our house with Della Robia and red bells and a Christmas tree with blinking lights. And, of course, my mother was shopping with determination. Sometimes, on Christmas Eve, she would need just a few more gifts, and the stock boys would carry packages out to her car.

Another memory is of the paging system, a doorbell-like device placed close to the ceiling of each floor. When someone was not in their office, they could be summoned with a simple ringing of their code, i.e., 2-1-2.

Denholms dressed up for the Christmas season.

Located on the street-floor balcony, Denholms had a rental library that loaned the book *The Egg and I* nineteen times. The sales slips consisted of four copies: the office copy, a thin tissue page for the salesperson's records, the yellow one for the customer and the delivery record. The customer's charge card was run through a device that would emboss his or her name and address on all four slips. At one time, the store had fifty-two thousand charge customers.

One notable aspect of Denholms was the loyalty of its employees. Those were the days when people hoped to get a job with a company they liked and stay as long as they could. Such was the membership of the Twenty-five-Year Club, a group of employees who had worked at Denholms for a quarter of a century. I believe there were even handfuls who may have claimed membership in the fifty-year mark.

And so I can say Denholms forever, and forever Denholms.

Directory	Previous Buyers
LOWER LEVEL	
Housewares	Mr. E. Randall
Restaurant	Mr. K. Kilceyne
Shoe Repair	Mr. T. Lion
Notions	Mrs. J. Denis
Budget Shoes	Mr. J. Syaschak
CHATHAM ANNEX	
Yard Goods, Silk, Wool, Cotton	Mrs. B. Sandberg
Sewing Machines	Mr. W. Potter
MAIN FLOOR	
Men's Furnishings	Mr. William Farrington
Men's Clothing	Mr. R. Davis
Books, Magazines	Mrs. Joudrey
Stationery and Cards	Miss M. Finney
Hosiery, Gloves Handbags	Miss M. McInerny
Handkerchiefs, Umbrellas	Miss M. McInerny
Women's Shoes and Slippers	Mr. I. Katz
Russell Stover Candy/ Gourmet Shop	Miss Dot Eagen
Watch Repair	Mr. H. LaVenture
Jewelry	Mrs. Kneeland
SECOND FLOOR	
Linen, Domestics	Mr. J. Nolan
Sleepwear, Underwear, Uniforms	Mrs. C. Morrissey

Directory	Previous Buyers
Housecoats and Budget Dresses	Miss Rose Brogan
Corsets, Brassieres	Mrs. C. Morrissey
THIRD FLOOR	
Boys' Department: Clothing, Boy Scouts, Varsity Shop	Mr. Tony Morello
Girls' Department, Pre-Teen	Mrs. Fleming
Infants, Infant Furniture	Miss Safer
Children's Shoes	Mr. Berliner
Capezio Shoe Shop	Mr. Bean
Better Dresses, Budget Dresses, Bridal Salon	Miss Elsie McCarthy
Misses and Women's Suits, Furs	Miss Elsie McCarthy
Better Coats, Budget Coats	Mr. Megathlin
Millinery, Wig Salon	Mr. R. Huskel
Sportswear, Blouses, Juniors	Mrs. Josephine Carbone
Budget Sportswear and Blouses	Mrs. Josephine Carbone
Young Junior Sportswear	Mrs. Josephine Carbone
FOURTH FLOOR	
Silverware, Men's Boutique	Mrs. Muriel LeClair
China, Glassware, Gifts	Miss Lillian MacNeil
Trim the Tree Shop	Miss Lillian MacNeil
Furniture, Bedding	Mr. A. DiTommaso
FIFTH FLOOR	
Photo Studio	Mrs. Fox
Wallpaper, Paint	Mr. Charles Kellogg

Directory	Previous Buyers
Draperies, Rugs	Mr. John McLoughlin
Lamps, Luggage	Mr. William Publicover
Records and Radios	Miss Midge Beach
Televisions	Mr. Russell Corsini
	Mr. Neske (assistant)
Cameras and Film	Miss Lorraine Sundquist
Pictures	Mrs. Hazel Fox
Art Needlework	Mrs. Florence Melanson
SIXTH FLOOR	
Beauty Salon	Mrs. F. Dolan

Denholm and McKay Company
484 Main Street
Worcester, Massachusetts, 01608
Phone Number: PL34721 and Enterprise 6111

Notes

CHAPTER 2

1. Collections of the Worcester Society of Antiquity, Vol. 2.

CHAPTER 3

2. *The American States Reports; Containing the Cases of General Value...* Vol. 12.
3. *Inland Massachusetts Illustrated* (Worcester, MA: Elstner Publishing Company, 1891).

CHAPTER 4

4. *Worcester Magazine.*
5. *The Standard Principal New England Losses,* January 29, 1921.

CHAPTER 5

6. *American Cloak and Suit Review.*

Chapter 6

7. *New York Times*, "Warn Dry Goods Men of Risk in Cheapness," 1932.
8. *Worcester Telegram and Gazette*, 1936.

Chapter 7

9. *Worcester Telegram and Gazette*, 1940.
10. *New York Times*, 1940.
11. *Worcester Telegram and Gazette*, 1943.
12. *New York Times*, 1943.
13. Worcester Public Library, 1946.

Chapter 8

14. *Worcester Telegram and Gazette*, 1951.

Chapter 10

15. Ibid., 1961.

Chapter 13

16. Ibid., 1968.
17. Worcester Public Library, 1969.

Chapter 14

18. *Worcester Telegram and Gazette*, 1971.

CHAPTER 15

19. Ibid., 1972.
20. Ibid., 1973.
21. *New York Times*, 1973.
22. Worcester Telegram and Gazette, 1973.
23. Ibid.
24. Ibid.
25. Ibid., 1974.
26. Ibid., 1975.

MEMOIRS BY PAT WOLF

27. *Worcester Daily Telegram*, 1944.
28. *Switchboard*, 1946,
29. *Evening Gazette*, 1973.